African Ways Again

More recollections of life in South Africa

By

Valerie Poore

A Rivergirlsbooks edition

ISBN: 9781977053213

Disclaimer

The contents of this book are the product of my recollections, and have both inaccuracies as a result of time passed and embellishments needed to turn a series of memories into readable stories. Names have been changed in the interests of discretion, although some people represented are referred to by their given names. As a result, if there are mistakes regarding the 'characters', the content or the time, I would like to make it clear that these are my errors and mine alone. In addition, please note I am a British writer and I use British spelling and grammar. This may sometimes differ from what US readers are accustomed to, so I hope those of you in the States will be indulgent with me on this.

Valerie Poore (January, 2018)

Dedication
This book is written in fond memory of
Peggy Bernard, Zeblon Dlamini,
Eunice Hattingh and Peter
It is also for
Hugh Rethman and Bev Nicholson

Contents

INTRODUCTION

In 2007, I published the original edition of African Ways, a memoir about living in rural South Africa. I wrote it because South Africa was getting a bad press in the world and I wanted to do something to give some balance to all the negative perceptions that were circulating. My aim was to let readers see the country and the people as I'd experienced them in the early eighties when fresh out from England, I arrived on a remote mountain farm in Kwa-Zulu Natal and learned to live a very different kind of life.

It was a dramatic change for my family and me. We'd been living in a society with every possible modern convenience and were suddenly transplanted to a fairly primitive existence judging by European standards. But we adapted and absolutely loved our three years in our rural African idyll. The people we lived among became very dear to us, and these were the characters that were the subject of the recollections in my memoir. At the end of those three years, my husband's employer transferred him to Johannesburg and it seemed like the right time to move to our own home. The upside was that since he travelled all over the country, where we actually lived didn't matter. Added to that, we didn't want to leave Natal. We had friends around us and our children had their own social circle as well, so we decided to look for a house nearby. We found one in the pretty settler village of Byrne some ten kilometres down the mountain from the farm.

African Ways ends without explaining this, and to many readers it seemed as if we had actually left South Africa. That was not the impression I intended to create although I will admit that leaving the mountain felt final in many ways. I never intended to write another book about my life in the area. For me, those first few years were so special and so rare that everything afterwards seemed to be less somehow. Part of it was, I suppose, because we moved on to a more 'normal' existence, but it would also be fair to say that the subsequent years involved some personal upheavals which were not much fun. These events coloured my memories. It wasn't easy to see the sunshine through the smog for a long time, and so a sequel was not even on my 'possibly' list. In fact, I actively resisted the idea of writing it because I didn't believe it would be a story worth telling.

This certainty faltered when readers of African Ways started asking me what happened next, and I began to mull it over. Then one day I was talking to the elder of my two daughters about the 'post farm period'. Jodie was just old enough to remember the move at the end of 1984 and the year that followed actually meant much more to her than our life on the farm. I suspect this was because it coincided with when she started school, a major event in a small person's life. As happens in such 'do you remember this?' sessions, we didn't always agree and almost had a few fierce arguments as we thrashed out what was true and what was fabrication in her fertile imagination – and if I'm honest, in mine too. Still, we realised there was plenty there in both our memories and the more we talked, the more we prodded and probed, and the more we both remembered. The result is this book, which begins with the purchase of our little house in the Byrne valley.

I should say upfront that ours was not an expat world, nor was it in any way glamorous; it was country life, African style. These were the last years of the apartheid regime, but in our small corner of Natal we were able to be largely non-political and to flout many of the rules. Being English born and recent imports we didn't know or even care much about what the laws were. Certainly all the time we were on the farm with our Dutch landlord and landlady, apartheid never seemed to impinge on our lives. We were foreigners, for sure, but we just saw ourselves as living among country people as others do who move to rural Greece, France or Spain. As for our way of life, it was just a simple existence and my family and I lived and interacted with South Africans of all races and hues. But for me, that's what gave it its colour and richness.

African Ways Again is for those who enjoyed the first book and who are interested in what happened next – or maybe just what being in South Africa was like in those days. I hope my recollections contribute to the picture I tried to build in my first memoir and although I would love to suggest it's necessary to read the two in sequence, I don't think it's true; all these stories are self-contained. I should also say that while I've done my best to check my facts, these haven't always been verifiable due to the time that has elapsed; details on record are often sketchy or lacking completely. Nor has it been possible to consult everyone I mention individually. I've had to accept that after all this time some of them may not even be alive today while most will have moved away. For this reason, many of the names of the people I've written about have been changed and sometimes even their physical appearance too.

The following chapters consist of a series of vignettes and anecdotes. They are more or less in chronological order and have more of a narrative than African Ways. The first half follows our move and our immediate post-farm life in the Byrne Valley. The second half covers the year and a bit we spent in Richmond, a small country town around forty-five kilometres from the provincial capital, Pietermaritzburg (otherwise referred to as 'Maritzburg). Inevitably, there will be references to certain places, events and people that I wrote about in the first book. After all, we lived in the same area, but in these cases I've added details and anecdotes I haven't mentioned before. While some of the stories focus on specific events, others are more general descriptions of our life at the time. It was a period of change and great challenge for me, a bittersweet time too. Nonetheless, I hope that when all's said and done, these recollections form a lively and entertaining account of the colourful people, places and events of my South African past.

BITING THE BULLET IN BYRNE

Bill and I stood in the sunroom of the cottage we'd come to view. We looked down the garden that stretched beyond the wide steps leading off the French doors in front of us. A plum tree spread its limbs to the right of the steps but further on there were pomegranate, apple, peach and orange trees. It was a veritable orchard enclosed by wooden post and rail fencing. About halfway down on the right stood a small shed tucked between two of the fruit trees. I shook my head, smiling in disbelief. It was gorgeous. Bill grinned happily too. The shed was a perfect man den.

Even better, there was an outdoor utility room where we could have, and I hardly dared even think the words, a washing machine. We hadn't owned one of those for more than three years as we were still living on the farm at the top of the mountain. Not that its location was a reason for the lack of basic amenities per se, but the farm had no electricity and we were used to all aspects of living off the grid. I loved it, except for one thing: washing by hand.

Having electricity would mean a return to normal life, something part of me regretted but the other part whooped with internal joy at the prospect of putting my laundry in a real, hi-tech, front-loading, many-programmed, fully-automatic washing machine. But this wasn't the only upside. The position of the cottage was an advantage too. It was in the tiny village of Byrne, known for its historical importance as being one of Natal's early settlements. Far enough out of town to be rural, it was still much closer to tar roads and civilisation than we'd been accustomed to. After weeks of viewing houses in and around Richmond, which was the nearest urban area of any size, this one was the first to strike a chord.

'What do you think?' Bill asked, dragging me back to the moment.

Turning away from the paradise outside and casting my eyes around the cottage again, I hesitated, seeing the somewhat minimal amenities with more practical eyes. The rose-tinted vision cleared.

'It's awfully small,' I said, suddenly filled with doubt.

'Yes, but I'll be away a lot, won't I? It'll be mostly for you and the girls.'

'I know, but even so, you'll be back at weekends and, well, there's only one bedroom.'

'True, but we can use bunks for the kids.'

I frowned. He didn't seem to get the problem. However, I wasn't going to say more as the seller, Jean, a charming single woman in her fifties, was standing with us and I wasn't quite ready to discuss our sleeping arrangements with someone I'd only just met. The idea of 'Hello, I'm Val and this is Bill and we want to sleep together without our children' seemed a little too direct. Still, we'd have to think about it before making a decision.

Unfortunately, Bill was in a rush as usual. He was starting a new job in Johannesburg in a couple of months and wanted us to be off the farm before he headed north. For my part, I didn't feel the need to hurry. I was

12

perfectly happy with our annex flat next to the main house up at Cottingham Farm, and I liked having the company of Ouma and Oupa Ellens, the Dutch couple who owned it. There was always someone to talk to; the girls adored Bongi, the Ellenses' Zulu maid; and there were always the farm children for them to play with. But Bill had a point. Jodie, the elder of our two daughters, was due to begin pre-school the following year. On the three days she'd be attending, I would need to drive into Richmond twice a day to take and fetch her, and the sand road up the mountain (a track bearing a close resemblance to a rocky river bed) was often hazardous when the weather was bad. Bill added more persuasive arguments.

'After driving six hundred kilometres from Jo'burg, the last thing I want is to get stuck in a mudslide on the last stretch,' he said.

'I suppose,' I answered, wondering why it was only an issue now. He'd already been working in Durban for a year and that was nearing a hundred and twenty kilometres each way. And he did that every day. He'd always managed the mudslide before and even thought it good fun; a good test of his driving skills, he said. I decided to counter argue.

'The thing is,' I reasoned, 'we don't want to find we've bought something we'll regret once we're tied into a mortgage.'

We were having this conversation as we drove back to the farm. I was filled with uncertainty. I loved the little white-painted cottage with its sunny lounge and bright kitchen. Byrne too was such an attractive place. It was like a traditional English village with its picket fences, flower-decked houses and winding lanes, but the issue of the single bedroom wasn't the only part that bothered me.

Currently, we were living on top of the mountain; in Byrne, we would be at its foot. I was used to forever views over rolling hills to the Drakensberg; in Byrne, there was no view except over the village and across to the 19th century church on the other side of the valley. The mountain would tower over us, and I wasn't sure how I would like that. All the same, the price was about as much as we could afford and I couldn't ignore the fact that the garden was a delight. There was also the added attraction of electricity at the flick of a switch and water on tap. I'd been without these facilities for so long I was beginning to think of them as luxuries.

'Okay,' I said eventually. 'Let's make an offer.'

'Excellent!' said Bill. 'Will you arrange it?'

'I will. I'll go into Richmond Estates tomorrow.'

Which I did.

It so happened that Jean, the owner of the cottage, was the administrative secretary at the agency charged with selling the house, so it was her I met when I popped into their office in Richmond the next day.

'Oh! Hello! I wasn't expecting to see you again so soon,' she smiled at me.

'Me neither,' I grinned back. 'But my other half is quite persuasive and he's decided we must make an offer. Should I do that with you?'

'Oh no, dear. That wouldn't be a good idea. We might come to blows,' she laughed. 'I'll get one of the agents to deal with it.' She got up, and then hesitated a moment. 'I don't suppose you want a job too, do you?'

'Who me?'

'Yes, dear. You see when I sell the house, I'll be moving away from the area and the boys will need someone to take my place. Can you type?'

'Um... sort of,' I replied. 'I used to type for my mother's business before I came to South Africa, but I haven't done any work since I've been here.' I didn't like to admit my typing was very much a two-fingered process.

'I'm sure you'd be fine, then. There's hardly anything to do really,' she went on with unnerving confidence. 'As long as you can answer the phone nicely and type a few letters, you can do the work. Even if you're a bit rusty, there's no pressure. The boys are very easy going,' she finished.

'And who are the boys?' I asked, imagining twelve-year-olds in shorts.

'Well, you must have spoken to one of them when you asked about viewing the house. That will have been Peter. I'll fetch him now. He'll be through the back making tea. The others will come in later. There's John, Gerald and Anthony.'

I chuckled. The gentleman I'd spoken to could hardly have been termed a boy, but so be it. Maybe the word was representative of how she treated them.

As if to confirm my thoughts, Peter followed Jean through the office like a lamb. I almost snorted. He might not have been a child, but he was still wearing shorts. Peter was a portly sixty something with a wonderful round, cherubic face. He had an even rounder girth and his shorts were held up by braces. I liked him on sight. He puffed his way over to a chair by the door. I had a feeling this was his place by the way he settled in, but it wasn't for long.

'So,' he began. 'You want to make an offer on Jean's place, do you?'

'Yes, we do.'

'Right then, we'd better go through to my desk and fill in some forms,' he smiled and got up again. Jean was already back behind her desk.

'Good luck,' she whispered. 'This might be your job interview too!'

The outcome of the purchase was that we not only took over Jean's house, but I took over her job as well. The offer for the house involved some simple paperwork and since we were prepared to pay the asking price, there was no need for negotiation. While Peter completed the blank spaces with our details on the pre-printed form, he asked me some questions.

'Where are you living now, Val?'

I told him. He wrote it neatly on the dotted line.

'How long have you been in the country?'

I told him that too.

'So you have a South African residence permit?' I nodded. 'That's good. Have you ever worked in an office like this?'

'No,' I admitted, 'but I'm used to answering phones and I've done a bit of office typing and admin.'

'Well, you've got a nice voice,' he beamed at me. 'Very proper and very English. I think you'll do. Anyway, if Jean likes you, that's good enough for us.' I'm sure I must have blushed, but I smiled my acceptance and we shook hands on it. And that was that.

Half an hour later, I left Richmond Estates with our offer already accepted barring Bill's signature and the prospect of a job for three mornings a week, providing John the senior partner agreed – which ultimately he did.

I barrelled back up the road to Byrne full of excitement. The village was on the way to the farm so to convince myself of the reality of what I'd just done, I drove round to the cottage to take another look. Situated close to a crossroads, it was the second house down in Charles Street and made a very good show of being everything that was cute, cosy and welcoming. The front fence was waist high and painted white; the windows were cottage-paned casements and the veranda along the front of the house gave it a quaintly colonial style. It wasn't old at all, though. It had been built about fifteen years previously and was nicely sturdy. Seeing it again like this, on my own, and without Bill pushing for a decision, I was much more at ease. Leaving Cottingham would still be a wrench but, I reasoned, it wasn't so far away and there were many aspects of life that would suddenly become much more convenient.

On the farm, we used oil lamps for light and gas bottles for cooking and heating water. None of this presented a problem and I came to enjoy the simple ritual of lighting the lamps every evening. However, if I wanted to iron Bill's shirts, I had to place old flat irons on the gas burner until they were hot enough to use. I became adept at doing my ironing this way, but it was hot work and needed constant care not to burn the clothes.

In our early days, quite a few of my skirts and jeans had interesting brown patches on them, and sometimes more than one; I always tested the iron on my own things before I risked Bill's work shirts; it didn't matter to me if I had burn patches in odd spots. Tie-dye wasn't completely out after all and I only had to worry about Bongi and Ouma laughing at my ineptitude. Eventually, I got used to it and knew exactly how long it took for the iron to reach the right temperature.

Even so, I wouldn't have any pangs about that part of our off-grid lives. Nor would I regret the frugal use of water, which was often a necessity if there was a drought. In Byrne, water would come through the pipes and be metered like town water; on the farm, we often had to go to the dam and fill up jerry cans to replenish our water tank. Turning back to the car, I got in and started on my way again. As I drove back to Cottingham I knew I would never live anywhere as special again, but with a few modern conveniences, I felt confident that life in Byrne would be bearable.

BUNKING DOWN

It didn't take us long to move the ten or so kilometres from the farm into Byrne; it was straight down the mountain, after all. We didn't have much in the way of possessions as the annex flat had already been furnished when we moved in, so apart from the fridge, the only appliance that belonged to us, it was just our clothes, our books, the children's toys and our two cats, Mitten and Foggy, that came too. The one thing I left behind was a piece of my heart. I would miss standing in the garden watching the folding foothills of the Drakensberg change from purple to gold depending on how the light hit them; I would miss seeing the snow caps on the peaks; and above all, I would miss Ouma, Bongi, and her father Khezwa, whose colour, wit and humour had enriched my life for the last three years. But sad as I was to leave, I knew it made sense. I had to make the best of the change and I initially channelled my energies into making our new house a home and getting used to having a job as well.

Given that we were starting from scratch in Byrne, our little house was, thankfully, easy to furnish. The veranda that extended the entire width of the front wall provided shade and a protected area from the rain. There was no hallway, as the front door opened straight into the lounge off which were the entrances to the other three rooms: the bedroom, sunroom and kitchen. As a result, there was little spare space and so furniture had to be kept to the essentials. Jean had gone for the traditional English country look with elegant, but old-fashioned polished oak tables and chairs alongside floral-patterned armchairs. Such a themed style was not something we could afford; nor would we want it, not being chintz and French polish type of people. In any event, we knew we would have to make do with what we could find.

The bedroom was quite large enough to accommodate a double bed as well as two bunk beds, which we put against one wall — it was the only solution despite my reservations about us all sleeping in one room. Even Jodie was not so keen. At the grand age of five, she knew what she didn't like.

'You won't snore too loud, will you Daddy?'

'What do you mean? I don't snore!'

'You do, you do, and you sound like Oupa's lawnmower,' she teased, giggling at his indignant expression.

'Well, you'll just have to put your fingers in your ears. Anyway, Mummy will poke me if I snore, won't you, Mummy?' He looked to me to play the part so I nodded, pretending enthusiasm despite knowing what kind of reaction I would get if I so much as dared to prod him awake.

'See?' Bill turned to Jodie. 'It won't last long even if I do,' he said, giving her a mock cuff on the ear. I just hoped his snoring was the only issue we'd have in sharing a room with the girls.

We bought all the beds on the 'never ever' from a furniture chain store famous for a jingle that cheerfully promised customers 'you've got an uncle in the furniture business'. This ditty naturally lulled the eager hire-purchaser into thinking everything the store sold was reliable, solid and safe from anything so nasty and inconceivable as repossession. In truth, hire-purchase was cripplingly expensive, but the company's marketing was good and so we signed our salaries away for what was probably about ten times the cost of a cash purchase. I vowed to pay it all off as quickly as possible.

In the fully carpeted lounge, we placed an L-shaped sofa unit and a coffee table, both bought from a second-hand furniture emporium in 'Maritzburg and transported on Oupa Ellens' *bakkie* (pick-up truck), which he kindly lent us since Bill had exchanged his Toyota Land Cruiser for his work car. A round, glass-topped dining table and chairs, also second-hand, went into the sunroom. This, together with a few bookcases and drawer units scavenged from various junk shops completed our hastily gathered furnishings.

The most difficult item to install was our monster fridge. For some time before we left the farm, we'd had this paraffin-fuelled giant, very fifties in design and terrifyingly efficient. We found it at an antique auction that was held at a nearby village cattle market once a month; fortunately, the cattle were not present on these occasions. The fridge was standing on its own amongst a heap of other sundry kitchen appliances, looking out of place and – well – huge. Bill saw it first.

'Val, look! There's a fridge like the Ellenses'.'

'So there is. It looks bigger than theirs, though. That one's massive!'

'Yeah,' he breathed. There was a rapturous shine in his eyes. 'Isn't it fantastic?'

Oh no, I thought. Here we go.

'Come and look at it with me,' he commanded.

So I hoisted my youngest, the still small Maryssa, into my arms, and we picked our way through old irons, kettles, toasters, electric mixers and broken radios to reach the mammoth. Bill inspected it minutely. Although distinctly grubby, everything was there, even the long shallow paraffin container with its adjustable wick that slotted into the fridge at the bottom.

'I want it,' said Bill, the voice of a fanatic having replaced his own. He'd been possessed. I'd heard that tone and seen the gleam before, mostly over motorbikes, but what the heck? Why exclude ancient, decrepit fridges from potential compulsive obsession?

'Right,' I said. 'I'll go and do the groceries while you wait to bid for it.' I knew this would take a while. Every single item in the auction, down to the last screw, was numbered and all the items were offered in ascending numerical order. The fridge was a very high number and I couldn't see either daughter standing meekly by while we waited for Bill to reach his nirvana.

When he'd finally achieved those celestial heights for a knock-down price (who in heaven would want such a beast anyway?), it took Bill and a hastily acquired team of helpers to manhandle it onto the Land Cruiser, which we still had at the time. The fridge worked a treat after he'd restored it to working order and I'd rendered it more hygienic. The only problem was that it weighed so much I could easily have believed it was lined with lead. I couldn't budge it at all on my own, so getting it down to the cottage involved another team of helpers; putting it in place was even more of an adventure. The space for a fridge was just inside the kitchen door.

We shuffled it through the lounge together but at the entrance to the kitchen, the fun started.

'We need to move it to the right,' called Bill from his side of the beast. 'Ready, steady, push!'

I couldn't see him, so I shoved it hard as instructed.

'That's not right,' he yelled.

'Yes, it is,' I retorted. 'It's my right.'

'Well, push it to my right, then!'

'You mean left?'

'That's right!'

'Huh?'

'I meant that's correct, silly, push left then!'

'Who are you calling silly? Just make your mind up!'

And so it went on. By the time we'd manoeuvred it into the very tight gap in the kitchen, we'd lost both our tempers and more than a few chunks of paint from the door frame. All the same, it was there and life could begin in earnest.

Within days of moving in, Bill took off for Johannesburg to start the new phase of his career, which left me free to settle in properly.

The first thing to get used to was being able to turn lights on and off at will. We'd built up a routine on the farm for lighting the oil lamps and it was something I'd become accustomed to. We lit them, we turned them up or down as needed, and then we extinguished them when we went to bed. Now, the risk was that we'd switch on lights and forget to turn them off. Electricity bills were the downside of all this instant energy and we had to get into the habit of not wasting it. With two small daughters who were fascinated by the magic of electricity, such care took some training. While they couldn't reach the switches for the ceiling lights, table lamps assumed a new purpose.

Entertainment. For the first few days, one or other of them would sit and play strobe lights with our lounge lamps until I caught them at it and curtailed the fun. But their delight in these new toys was infectious. I wanted to do it too.

The other new compulsion was the phone. At Cottingham, we didn't have our own phone and only used the Ellenses' old-fashioned wind-up phone on the party-line they shared with everyone else along the road to Elandskop. When I think about it, the girls had quite possibly never seen a normal telephone before and we rarely used the Ellenses' in any event. Now we had a modern instrument with a smooth dial and normal handset of our very own. It was the first thing Bill made sure of before we moved so we could keep in touch while he was away. Our gleaming new communications system sat on a low occasional table near the front door to be close to the incoming line. And it was there, sitting on the floor next to it, that I found the girls on several occasions pretending to have conversations with their friends. At least I hope they were pretending. I hadn't shown them how to make a call, but it didn't stop them from inventing very realistic scenarios to play out.

Jodie and Mo, which is what Maryssa was more generally known as, loved the new garden too, especially Jodie. Her imagination blossomed as she scampered out in the morning to inspect the dewdrops on the long grasses. I liked to watch her and encouraged her fascination for all things natural.

'Did you know those drops are where the fairies sleep?' I asked her.

'Do they? I never see any fairies in them,' she said, peering into the droplets.

'That's because they've already gone to their next jobs long before you're awake, sweetie. After all, tooth fairies have to collect the teeth and leave a coin before the little girls and boys wake up and that's really early,' I said, emphasising the last two words.

The stream that flowed past the bottom of the garden was also an endless fascination. It was just a brook at this point, being both shallow and narrow. Tumbling over a sandy bed, it flowed into the river Serpentine at the bottom of the hill. One of the couples we'd known in the valley for some time before moving were Alex and Bruce who grew citrus on a small farm that bordered the road just outside Byrne. They had a little boy much the same age as Jodie. Once we'd settled in, young Harry came to play quite frequently, and he and Jodie spent happy hours paddling in it. They squished their feet in the sand, scooped 'desert' islands into shape with plastic spades and watched the water rush round their ankles before returning to the kitchen knee-high in mud. They were convinced there was a water sprite there that watched over them; I, on the other hand, knew it was only safe as long as there'd been no heavy rain, and even then, I wouldn't let Mo go and paddle unless I was with her.

As we'd moved in during the summer, the fruit trees were a further source of delight. On the farm, we'd just had a lemon tree, which I was already missing. But in our cottage garden, the plethora of windfalls from the plum, apple and peach trees kept the girls in free, healthy snacks right up until the winter. There was only one problem: snakes.

We'd only been there a month or so before we found that the village wasn't only bounded by a river called Serpentine, it had another serpentine connection of the worst kind. Mitten our tortoiseshell prima donna was famous for her war on snakes. Up at Cottingham, she'd not only brought in a steady stream of decapitated grass snakes, but she'd also seen off a large puff adder the girls and I had nearly stepped on. It was lying basking in the winter sun on the sand road where we were walking and in my dreamy state of gazing at the sky, I hadn't seen it. Mitten pounced on the fatly coiled snake, frightening the life out of the poor thing and sent it scurrying off into the undergrowth. I say 'poor thing' in hindsight, of course. At the time, I was rigid with the shock from what the children and I had so barely avoided; a puff adder's bite is deadly if not treated in time, and we were a long way from the nearest help.

After the move, Mitten and our tabby cat, Foggy (so named because we'd found her on the road one very foggy night) settled in well and before long, Mitten was once again queen of her realm. I noticed one day that she was peering with intense interest at a gap in the bricks at the bottom of the steps. She started dabbing at the hole and then crouched down to watch. There was clearly something in there, so I watched too, never suspecting what would emerge. Nothing happened so Mitten, still crouching and wriggling her bottom in anticipation, dabbed at the opening again. This time she got a reaction. A long, slender greyish form shot out of the hole with astonishing speed. Mitten gave chase but it disappeared before she could catch it. From its colouring, I knew it was a herald snake and was harmless, but I still didn't like the idea of having snakes so close to home. It later transpired the snake had made its nest there, so we let Mitten sit on guard as much as she liked and eventually she caught and beheaded them all with chilling efficiency, gruesome cat that she was. I have to say I was quite relieved.

Much more worrying, though, was the day Mo spotted a villainous looking green snake in the apple tree next to the shed. The frightening thing about it was that it was so well camouflaged I hadn't seen it all. It draped itself over the branches and between the leaves with just its head hanging down.

'Mummy, look!' Mo pointed, giggling. 'It's a tree snake!' The creature gave her a withering look and started to drop its head. I gasped in horror.

'Mo, come here! Right! Now!'

My daughter looked at me in surprise. She wasn't used to my being quite so peremptory. She didn't move, but the snake did. It dropped its head still lower regarding her with its venomous and evil eye.

Not waiting further, I dived and grabbed Mo, pulling her back to me with as much speed and force as I could. She didn't know what the snake was, but I did. It really was a tree snake, or *boomslang* as it is known – one of the most poisonous snakes in South Africa. A bite from that evil creature would have seen my little one in serious trouble, and maybe even dead. We withdrew to what I deemed a safe distance and watched as the *boomslang* pulled itself back onto its branch and then slithered higher up into the tree. I knelt down in front of Mo.

'Never, never stand under that tree, Mo. Promise me.'

'Why?'

'Because that tree snake is very, very bad. And if it bites you, you will be a very sick Momo,' I said with all the seriousness I was able to load into my words. Mo looked at me.

'What about Jojo, Mummy? Will the tree snake bite her

too?' I was a little perplexed at her almost gleeful look.

'Yes, sweetie. It will. So we must make sure she doesn't stand under it either. Snakes are very shy so maybe it will go away but until it does, don't go near the tree. Okay?'

'Okay... I'll go and tell Jojo.' And she ran off on her chubby little legs, shouting, 'Jo, Jojo, there's a bad snake in the tree! It's going to bite you! Come and see! Quick!'

I shook my head in exasperation. Sibling antagonism was something I was already used to but antagonism with murderous intent was something else.

THE CANNONBALL RUN

Having a car or pick-up (*bakkie* in local parlance) was vitally important in such a rural area. There was no public transport at all and with the condition of the roads varying according to the weather, tough and sturdy was more important than comfortable and elegant. When we'd first arrived in Natal, I'd borrowed the Ellenses' Datsun *bakkie* while Bill was at work. They'd been away on a long trip at the time, but since their return we'd been through a series of second-hand cars, most of which didn't survive long on the rough roads. The four-wheel-drive Toyota Land Cruiser we'd had for a while was ideal as was the old Datsun, the brand that became Nissan in later years.

By the time we moved we each had our own vehicles. Bill's was courtesy of the upmarket German automotive company he was working for and was definitely on the classy side, although under all that shiny metallic paint was some stout and reliable engineering. Mine was a somewhat special 'classic'. It was a dirty white Citroen GS hatchback that we bought in Durban for the princely sum of just over a hundred Rands. Riddled with rust from the salty humid maritime air, I knew it wasn't going to survive our rough road conditions all too long, but it was a wonderful vehicle and I cherished it. Its very special feature was its hydraulic suspension. On the rutted and rarely graded roads up to the farm, I could raise the suspension from its normal low position to a much higher level to avoid bashing the sump on the rocks and craters chiselled out by torrents of water when the rains came. Sometimes, when the steep sections of the track were knee deep in mud from heavy downpours, I would adjust it by means of a lever from the lowest to the highest level (admittedly not recommended by the manufacturers except for changing tyres) and turn off the road onto the mountain slopes. Then we would drive across country, over the hills, humps and ditches until we could reach a drier section of road further on.

'Go, Mum, go,' the girls would squeal with excitement as we bounced over terrain that even four-wheel-drive vehicles hesitated to try.

My attitude became pretty much the family's personal cliché: 'if you run out of road, then make your own.'

Without the adjustable suspension, there was no other way we could have made it and we often left other, less versatile cars stranded, waiting for tractors or four-wheel-drive trucks to pull them out of the mire. Riding high on its pumped-up hydraulics, the old Citroen handled it all with ease – although it didn't do anything to extend its active life, as we were to find out later on.

Another source of extreme delight for Jodie and Mo was the famous 'cannonball run', a hair-raising but thrilling ride we would take from the top of the mountain almost all the way into Richmond without putting the car into gear. We sometimes had to do this when money was short, but as often as not, we did it for the sheer fun of it. As with our off-road excursions, it was only possible when the Citroen had its suspension raised. I used to drive over the crest of the first hill on the way from the farm and then slide the gear lever into neutral. We would then coast down the mountain allowing the bends and rises to take the speed off the car before it became a complete runaway. The girls used to shriek with excited terror as we gathered speed, only to yell with disappointment if we slowed down or, heaven forbid, nearly came to a halt on a rise.

'Come on, car, come on!' they would shout, jumping up and down on the back seats as if to urge our old banger on.

I used to get as much of an adrenaline rush as they did and loved the sheer nonsensical joy of it. Of course, we would sometimes be frustrated by meeting another car on the road, but most of the time, we could resume our rollercoaster journey into town from the top of the next rise, revelling in the magnificent cloud of dust we left behind us as we hurtled down the hills.

With our new home in Byrne being so much closer to the main road, the cannonball run was much curtailed, but we still did it. The new test was to see if we could turn onto the final, tarred section and make it into Richmond without stopping. Since this last stretch was largely downhill and fairly well maintained, it was not so difficult to keep the car moving, but it still gave rise to lots of satisfied whoops when we rolled into town without having used so much as a sip of fuel.

The rewards of all this abuse were reaped a few months after we'd moved when the Citroen started showing signs of distress. Firstly, the alternator died and the battery no longer loaded while I was driving; I had to take it out every night and put it on a charger indoors. If I didn't, it would simply go flat, giving me a panic attack on the mornings I had to go to work. The other problem was definitely the result my extreme off-road rallying. After more than two years of pounding around in the bush during the rainy season, the highest setting on the suspension would no longer work; or rather it would go up, but gradually sink back to the middle setting. It got to the point where even the girls were complaining.

'Mummy, can we go bundy-bashing... please?' Mo whined one day. 'Bundy' was her version of *bundu*, the Bantu or African word for a wild, uninhabited place. They'd picked up several Zulu words and phrases while playing with the farm kids but adjusted them to their own versions. Naturally, *bundu*-bashing was what I called our driving adventures.

'Not today, sweetie,' I said. 'The car's a bit tired and doesn't like it anymore.'

Although it was wet and slippery, I couldn't risk any serious sump skimming, a decision that didn't meet with either daughter's approval, so I slithered slowly up the long hill that led us into Byrne with a chorus of moans issuing from the back seat. That was really the end. I complained to Bill the next time he came home. He nodded, but other than that said nothing.

A few weekends later, just before my thirtieth birthday, he told us we were going on an outing as a treat. It was a beautiful autumn morning with vivid blue skies and golden light, a wonderful day for a trip out. We all piled into his fancy saloon and breathed in the scent of new leather. Bill drove so much he was given a new car every forty thousand kilometres. This was his second or maybe even third since he'd started working for the company just over a year before. It was such a change from my clunky car, I was both envious and grateful for at least a brief spell of luxury.

'Where're we going, Daddy?' 'How long will it take?' 'Are we nearly there?' came the chirrups from the back.

'Not far now,' said Bill, knowing full well the children had no clue about distance or time; they were a bit like a pair of puppies in that sense.

Just under two hours later, we arrived in Estcourt, a town north-east of Pietermaritzburg. It seemed an odd destination, an unlikely place for a birthday outing, until we turned into a car dealer's courtyard. I knew this was one of Bill's clients and I'd met Ali, the Indian dealer principal before. He was a round and cheerful soul and when he came to greet us, he was beaming more than usual.

'Good morning, Valerie,' he said, shaking my hand vigorously. 'Happy birthday! I am thinking we have a very nice surprise for you,' he went on, almost quivering with chuckles and pleasure. 'Would you come this way, please?'

It was then I realised he and Bill were in cahoots. My husband was chuckling too.

Ali led us around the back of the dealer's showroom and there I saw my new car for the first time. It was a very small, silver-grey Suzuki minibus, bearing a strong likeness to those tiny individual loaves of bread that are sometimes served for hotel breakfasts. And it was far too cute for anything. I gasped.

'That's for me?'

Bill was still chuckling, full of his pleasure at having kept the secret.

'Yep. It's all yours,' he grinned. 'Happy birthday, Val.'

Jodie and Maryssa were awestruck. They couldn't believe it either.

'It's like a little bread loaf!' breathed Jodie, gazing at its high roof and compact shape.

'Maybe half a loaf?' said Bill, knowing full well that this was what the car industry in South Africa had dubbed it.

The one disadvantage was that the arrival of the half-loaf sounded the death knell for the Citroen, but I felt it wasn't ready to die just yet and it received a welcome stay of execution. Alex, our friend from the citrus farm nearby, was suddenly left without a car when her old *bakkie* suffered a terminal breakdown. Transport in these remote areas was essential as I well knew, but the roads were not kind and Alex's Peugeot *bakkie* had rattled along them just one kilometre too far.

'What am I going to do, Val?' she asked when she called me, not yet knowing about my wonderful present. 'I have to go into Richmond for supplies every day now. We've just employed more guys to plant trees and we're always needing something for them.'

Alex and Bruce grew mostly oranges and were working hard to build up their orchards. Their farm wasn't large, but at certain times of the year, it was quite labour intensive.

'Well,' I grinned into the phone. 'As it happens, I might be able to give you a temporary solution.'

I explained why my old Citroen was now surplus to requirement. I also gave her full details of all its problems.

'But,' I said, 'it will get you out of trouble for the moment, and give you time to look for another car.'

'Oh Val, that would be great! I don't care what it's like as long as it stops and starts!'

'Well, let's just hope it starts before it stops,' I laughed. 'Shall I come and fetch you? You can just drive it away,

34

then.'

'Fantastic! You're a lifesaver!'

'Just remember it's not new. You're actually saving the car's life. It was about to be condemned.'

Even that didn't put her off and she just laughed. When I collected her shortly after her call, I told her how pleased I was she could use it. I hated the idea of scrapping my stoic old chariot.

'That makes two of us, Val,' she assured me. 'I don't know what I'd have done without you.'

As she backed the car out of the garden an hour later, I waved it a sad goodbye, not knowing then how short its remaining time would be.

Just one week later, Alex called me again.

'The Citroen's suspension has collapsed completely,' she said. 'I came out this morning and the whole car was sitting on the ground... well almost.' She sighed dramatically.

'Oh Alex, I'm so sorry! If I'd known it was going to go so soon, I'd never have offered it to you.'

'Ach it's not so *lekker*, but it's not your fault. You *did* tell me it was on its last legs.' *Lekker* was the all-in-one Afrikaans word for anything nice. We all used it.

'I know, but I never thought it would give up quite so quickly. Can I help you get rid of it?'

'*Nee*,' she said. 'Not to worry. Bruce'll give it to his guys. They'll strip it and sell the bits, I'm sure.'

She was being pragmatic, I knew, but I felt terrible about it. All the same, it crossed my mind that after all its sterling service to me, my trusty old steed felt I'd abandoned it and in the sorrow of neglect, with no more 'bundy-bashing' and cannonball runs, it had just sighed and died.

NEIGHBOURS AND HELPERS

Byrne village was founded by settlers back in the late 1840s. The settlers came by boat from England as 'approved' emigrants brought to Natal by one JC Byrne & Co., a company that also offered its passengers designated parcels of land in a number of areas. One of these was the Byrne Valley, named after the man himself. There was a problem, though. Apparently, Mr Byrne had never physically been to 'his' valley before encouraging emigrants to go there and it seems his ideas about what the terrain was like were completely mistaken. This was not country suited to crop growing, and it is said that some of the settlers were so disappointed when they saw what they were getting they didn't take up the offer. After all, there were other 'Byrne settlements' they could go to, so why stay? Richmond, with environs much better suited to agriculture, was also originally populated by settlers brought out by Mr Byrne.

By the time we arrived in the valley some hundred and thirty years later, the boundaries of the village were well marked and all the stands, those individual parcels of land promised by Mr Byrne, were carefully demarcated. It amazed me then, and still does, that land registry in South Africa was so well established considering how undeveloped so much of the country was. Anyone wanting to find out who owns a piece of land pretty much anywhere in the country can find it registered at the Deeds Office complete with diagrams, dimensions and deed holders. An application to do a 'Deeds Office Search' will provide the searcher with the records of past and present owners as well as all the relevant information about rights of way, boundaries and services – or at least it did in the 1980s.

But getting back to Byrne, there were two main thoroughfares that ran through the village. Leading off the through-route to Elandskop, the first road, Market Street, followed the gradient of the hill round until it bisected Charles Street, which ran from the upper to the lower village. I use the word 'road' a bit pretentiously here as in reality they were no more than bumpy dirt and stone tracks, but they were the main streets off which the smaller side streets led. At the top end of the village, the road ended at the entrance to a forestry area; at the bottom, it was halted by the small river that was known rather grandly as the Serpentine. The whole settlement of Byrne lay on the lower slopes of the ridge that formed the backbone of the mountain on which we had lived since arriving in South Africa. Byrne was in its valley, a green and pleasant place to build a community but without much arable land on which to grow things. It developed instead as a residential area, its only real claims to village status being the church and a trading store.

Living there felt very safe. I never saw the need to lock doors or worry about theft. We'd never had any problems on the farm either. Walking alone or being at home alone with everything wide open was normal and something we never thought about. At the time, the Byrne Valley and our mountain seemed to be in a bubble of stability although we used to hear about faction fights in rural villages several kilometres away. We were always told these conflicts were more clan-based than tribal; in other words, very local rivalries between *kraals* (small African settlements). They were quite frequent and sometimes violent, but they didn't affect us in our area. Byrne seemed even more secure given that we were surrounded by other houses.

When we moved there most of the stands were built on, but there were still quite a few empty spaces. The one next to our cottage was owned by a Christian minister, Father Muller. Whether he was Catholic or not, I'm not sure, but we always called him 'Father'. He had no house but he had a caravan where he used to stay when he could get away from his duties in the Ndaleni township, a sprawling location outside Richmond populated largely by the Zulus. Father Muller was German and even in this place so far from his original homeland he followed his country's national reputation for neatness and order when it came to his personal caravan site. I found it quite touching that he was fanatical about keeping his grass trimmed and his fruit trees pruned. I liked Father Muller very much and we enjoyed many a philosophical conversation over cups of coffee in our sunny lounge. He was a good neighbour.

He interested me because he claimed to be a confirmed socialist with strong communist leanings and I remember asking him how that worked with his position as a clergyman.

'It's easy,' he told me. 'Being both a practicing Christian and a socialist is no conflict at all. Christianity is only socialism with a forgiving side. All the other principles are much the same.'

That made me smile. It was so much his style and I didn't know enough about either doctrine to argue anyway; he was much more erudite than I was. I learned later that the author Graham Greene held similar ideas, so maybe it wasn't such an unusual position for Father Muller to take. That aside, I thought he was an example of his faith and his beliefs. He spent his days in Ndaleni where he ministered to his African flock in what I imagine was a no-nonsense style since that was the impression he gave me of his attitude. He was not a mild-mannered man at all and he was pretty direct in his speech, but for all that he had a ready smile and was very indulgent with the children – when he wasn't mowing his garden to within a millimetre of its life. Above all, he loved to talk and preach spiritual wisdom, which was rather like practical philosophy in riddles.

'Life is what you make it, Valerie,' he told me one day in his heavily accented English. 'And what you make of this life will help you in the next one. And,' he went on, wagging his finger at me, 'whether you like it or not, there will be a next one, so do your best to make this one as worthwhile as possible.' Then he smiled his quick smile and took himself off.

As far as helpers were concerned, I had a young Zulu woman in to look after the children on the days I had to work at Richmond Estates. Her name was Lindiwe. She worked for other people in the village too, but Monday, Wednesday and Friday mornings were for me. Lindiwe was a very different personality from Bongi, the Ellenses' maid; she'd been large, confident and jolly. By contrast, Lindiwe was small, shy, softly-spoken and gentle.

I first saw her waiting by the front gate one morning shortly after we'd taken up residence. The house was set well back from the front fence making the distance to the front door about twenty metres, so talking to her from there would have been uncomfortably loud. I never quite managed to adopt the local custom of bellowing across the valleys, so I walked over to greet her. She was wearing the customary maids' uniform of a brightly coloured housecoat with a matching apron and headscarf; hers was blue.

'Hallo, are you looking for someone?' I asked.

'Yes, madam, I am looking for work.'

'Ah, okay. Not someone, but something,' I said as much to myself as to her.

'Sorry, madam?'

'It doesn't matter. What work is it you want?'

'Maybe some mornings? I can clean,' she said, her eyes hopeful. 'Maybe madam work too? Then I look after the children?' It sounded like chil-*dren*.

I looked over my shoulder at the toys lying around the garden. Good clues.

'Hmm, that's a not a bad idea,' I smiled. 'What is your name?'

She told me and so opening the gate, I invited her in to chat about what arrangements we could make.

As she lived in Ndaleni, Lindiwe hitched a lift to her work in Byrne. This said so much to me about the symbiosis of all the people in the area. That she could rely on being at work on time every day just by getting a lift from a passing driver was quite a testament to the way society in the area worked. From my own experience, I was used to stopping on the road and picking up people walking into Richmond and back. It was just what we did, but I'd never thought about the implications for them if we didn't.

Lindiwe also told me her husband worked in the mines in Johannesburg and that she had four children. She looked after them on her own and reading between the lines, I understood that support was not all that forthcoming from Papa. I hired her to help me, but I was aware that she needed the help too. It would benefit us both and I knew it would take a load off my mind to have someone to care for Jodie and Mo while I was away. I just wondered who cared for hers, but I didn't like to pry too much.

The arrangement worked well for quite some time. Lindiwe came at eight in the morning just as I was leaving. She had a good breakfast of 'mealie pap' (maize porridge), bread and jam, although I'm sure she shared this with Jodie; my child had loved African food from the day she first tasted it and never missed an opportunity to dip into a bowl of pap. Lindiwe would then wash the dishes, tidy up and take care of the girls until I came home.

After a time, though, Jodie started nursery school in Richmond. She'd been going to one on a farm near Elandskop, but it was too far to take her there. In any event, she'd blotted my copybook with the teacher who ran it by repeating something she thought I'd said that wasn't complimentary to said teacher at all – it was all down to an unfortunate pronoun shift when 'it's a pain' became 'she's a pain'. Not good for my popularity ratings. As this was Jodie's second *faux pas* with the farm nursery school (the first being when she decided to tell her playmates I locked her in a cupboard whenever she was naughty), I was too embarrassed to take her back. Finding a larger and very welcoming play school in Richmond to which she could go on the days I was working was a great relief.

This event happened to coincide with Lindiwe developing a terrible cough. I couldn't help noticing it and as it got worse, I became worried. Tuberculosis was rife in South Africa and was said to be the biggest killer of any disease, associated as it was with poverty and malnourishment. Quite apart from being concerned about her health, I was also troubled about Lindiwe's close proximity to my little ones, neither of whom had previously been inoculated against TB. Children in South Africa are inoculated at birth, but mine were both born in the England where the jabs are only done when children are older, at age twelve. We'd been very lucky it hadn't been an issue before but it was now.

One morning when she arrived, I tackled her.

'Lindiwe, I think you must see the doctor about your cough.'

'Ah, madam, I no see doctor. No money for doctor.'

I knew that she was supporting her family on her own, so I was expecting something like this.

'Don't worry,' I told her. 'I will take you to the doctor in Richmond. I will pay. You look after me and my children, so now I look after you, okay?'

She smiled a little sadly. I expect she had mixed feelings about going to the doctor's. If she had any idea what was wrong, she would be forced to confront it.

'Okay, madam.'

That afternoon, after leaving the girls with Alex, I took her into town to the surgery. Having reassured the receptionist I would cover the cost, I went off to do some shopping at the supermarket and returned for her later.

The news was not good.

The surgery was also a dispensary in those days, and Lindiwe was waiting armed with what looked like a small heap of medicine boxes. Giving the pile an anxious glance, I suggested she go out to sit in the car while I settled the bill. Once she'd gone, I asked the receptionist for a diagnosis.

'I'm afraid Lindiwe has most likely got TB,' she said, confirming my fears. 'The doctor's taken some blood and we'll be sending it off to the lab, but I should warn you it's almost certain she has it.'

'Oh no! That's awful! She's got four kids to support!'

'Yes, I know. She told me. But it doesn't necessarily mean she won't survive. Now we know, we can treat her and with good food and the right medication, she could well recover.'

'And what about us? What about my two? They haven't had the jabs. Are they at risk?'

It sounded self-centred, even to me, but I had to ask.

'If they've been with her for some time, and aren't showing any signs of infection, then they'll probably be okay. TB is as much about living conditions and diet as it is about infection. Keep feeding them well, keep them healthy and they'll doubtless be just fine. Just avoid them having too much close contact with her, and make sure they have their injections next time around,' she finished.

That relieved me no end. The plus side of starting life on the farm with its pure air and wall-to-wall sunshine was that my daughters were so healthy neither of them had been to the doctor for anything more than routine jabs. The minus side was that we were living in a country known for widespread tuberculosis, and I didn't want to expose them to undue risk; I cringed when I thought of how close they'd been to Lindiwe already. It was bad enough that I'd left it this long. I spoke to the nursery school about Mo starting there too, and although she wasn't yet four they were quite amenable. That meant when Lindiwe was at the house they would both be away. It also meant I could continue to employ her as long as she was strong enough to do a bit of hoovering and tidying up. Problem solved. I knew Lindiwe desperately needed the money, meagre though it was.

Unfortunately, there was a going rate for maids' wages that I dared not outdo. This was something I'd learnt from one of my neighbours on the farm. She told me all the maids in the area earned the same amount and it just wouldn't do for me to try and increase it myself, however small the sum. It seems I would honestly have started a revolution had I paid more than was expected, not only among the employers but among the maids too.

I also remembered that another farm neighbour who employed a large workforce in his forestry business had tried to increase the men's pay believing this would motivate them more and cut down on absenteeism. His generosity backfired when the day after they collected their money, half of them didn't turn up for work. From what he surmised, they felt they'd been paid more than enough so didn't need to work for the next few days. Call it African logic but I wasn't going to risk contravening any rules, unwritten though they might be.

The only way to increase a maid's pay was by other methods, so to supplement the money she earned, I gave Lindiwe the girls' outgrown clothes as well as food, which incidentally was what nearly all employers in the area did too. Added to that, I paid towards her medicines. Although there was a state hospital she could go to where the costs charged were based on the patient's means, this would involve a long fifty-five-kilometre trek into 'Maritzburg, the provincial capital and an even longer wait in the outpatients' queues. It was both kinder and more efficient to make use of our own services. While apartheid was still legally in force at the time, my doctor was prepared to adapt whatever the rules were regarding segregation of treatment. As far as I know, this accommodating attitude was not unusual in rural areas providing there was a guarantee of payment, although I think the fees were still based on the patient's income.

'In a nutshell, as long as you give her the means, she can have the meds,' the doctor pointed out with a grin.

Even so, the costs couldn't have been that high as I don't remember finding them a burden, but then it's possible her other employers helped out too; another example of what we 'just did' then. There may have been going rates for pay along with the other injustices of apartheid, but it didn't mean we couldn't find workarounds when we wanted to.

FRIENDS AND FRIGHTS

Our little house in Charles Street was close to the crossing with Market Street. At the far end of Market Street, the road dwindled into a track ending at a farm-in-the-making belonging to the White family. Doris White became a very good friend to the girls and me and as Bill spent so much time away, it was a blessing to have such a caring companion so close by. She wasn't the cheerful, practical grandma type that Ouma was, but she was very kindly – perhaps more of an aunt than a mother. Her husband Dan was a decent soul but since he was always very busy trying to get the farm off the ground, we rarely saw him other than passing by on his tractor. The couple had a good-looking son of around twenty-five. His name was Mike, and for all his athletic physique, blonde hair and muscular tanned arms, he was very gentle and patient with the girls; something that surprised me given his age and sports star appearance. Mike helped out on the farm some of the time, but he was following some kind of diploma in business studies at a college in 'Maritzburg, so he wasn't at home to help his father that much during the day.

In any event, if he was there when we used to walk up to see Doris, Mike would take Jodie off to see their animals. It was quite comical to see the way my daughter worshipped him, and it made me smile to see her small hand clutching his big beefy one as she skipped along beside him. Having left the farm on the mountain where there were always cows, calves and chickens to watch, we missed being surrounded by agricultural as opposed to domestic animals. A visit to the Whites' calf and pig-pens was a great treat as a result.

Like their farmland, the family's house was in a state of semi-construction and poor Doris bore the trials of living in a building site with somewhat pained forbearance. About the only room that was even remotely finished was the kitchen, and even that was only bare plastered walls – plus the basic framework of what would eventually be fitted cupboards.

Doris was Scottish and still had the lilting accent from her country of origin; Dan and Mike were hundred percent South African with the clipped vowels and intonation I'd become used to after nearly four years in the country.

'Howzit, Val,' they would shout as I walked past.

'Fine, thanks!' I'd call back. 'And you?'

'*Ja*, well, no fine!' would come the response, the major emphasis being on the '*ja*' and 'fine'.

This, I'd discovered, was an odd but typical South African response to pretty much anything. I have no idea where it came from or how it started, but there were many of these combi Afrikaans-English expressions. For instance, if you finished a job and were ready to go somewhere else, you'd announce you were 'finish *en klaar!*', this last being the Afrikaans word for both 'finish' and 'ready'. It would also be the signal to whoever was listening that you could leave. Then in a restaurant at the end of the meal, you might 'pay and *rij*' (pronounced 'ray'), meaning you could settle the bill and *rij* (drive) away.

In any event, Dan and Mike had all of these South Africanisms and more, while Doris remained traditionally Scottish in every way.

'Hellooo, Val,' she greeted me every time we went there. 'Would you care for a wee cup of tea?'

I would usually accept even though she knew I only drank coffee. We would head into her slightly gloomy, unfinished kitchen and I'd sit down at the deal table, hoisting Mo onto my knees.

'How are the bairns?' she always asked, as she filled the kettle and put it on the stove.

It was like a formula we had to go through at each meeting. She could see my 'bairns' were both bristling with health, but somehow we couldn't get any conversation going until I'd assured her they were healthy and happy.

She would then make me a cup of Ricoffy, the instant coffee and chicory mix favoured in South Africa. It had been hard to get used to at first. I didn't really like chicory, but there didn't seem to be anything much else that was affordable and anyway, it was what everyone drank; that or another similar brand called Koffiehuis. I could only drink Ricoffy white and it actually tasted good with a good slug of home-produced, full-cream, unpasteurised milk. But I rather think it was more a case of having a dash of coffee with my milk than the other way round.

The plasterwork in Doris' kitchen was a sort of terracotta colour and there was only one window that looked out onto a jungle of greenery; hence the feeling of darkness. The rest of the house was a jumble of half-

48

finished walls, woodwork and cables. Nonetheless, I admired the family for their pioneering spirit as they'd bought the land as a vacant plot and built everything up themselves; or at least Dan had with a bit of help from his son and a few part-time workers. I don't know what Mike thought of it all, but I don't think Doris was very happy there.

As I recall, they'd sold a spacious, comfortable home in Durban to start a new life in the country and she found it hard to adjust to the inconvenience and discomfort of these early beginnings in Byrne. There were also times when Dan was short-fused due to the many frustrations of trying to grow crops, employ workers who were not always reliable, and build a house from scratch. I suspect Doris took the brunt of this; her demeanour was one of tired acceptance. I liked to think we brought a little *joie de vivre* into her world. At least, I think the children did.

Through the densely wooded area I could see beyond the kitchen window was a large pond, or small lake, depending on how you define each of these. It had wonderful clean water and best of all, most of it was shallow and made a great paddling pool. In the middle, though, the ground fell sharply away and it was very deep. Doris encouraged me to take the girls there to cool off in the heat of the summer months – 'for a wee dip' as she put it – as long as I kept a close eye on them and didn't let them go too far from the bank.

Talking of heat, Byrne could be like an oven. Being in the valley, the sun's warmth was sucked in and trapped between the high ridges that surrounded it. It wasn't unusual for the temperature to rise to 40 degrees in the early months of the year. The air was stifling with an oppressiveness we never experienced on Cottingham, the Ellenses' mountain farm. Our summers there had been sparkling, the intensity of the sun tempered by the freshness of the altitude. Down in Byrne, we wilted and it was a great relief to take the girls up to the Whites' small lake.

On one occasion, I took Alex and Bruce's son, Harry, with us too. The girls knew they had to keep close to the sides; the surface of the water was about fifty metres across, so even accounting for the deep part, there was plenty of playable space. But despite telling five-year-old Harry about the danger in the middle, he either didn't listen or simply forgot. I wouldn't like to think he chose to disobey me, but I suppose that's a possibility too.

In any event, when we arrived, I stripped down to my bikini and settled myself down on the grassy bank with a book while the small things played around in the shallows. It was deliciously cool there, protected as we were by the tall, over-arching trees, and it wasn't long before I was immersed in my reading. I don't know quite what it was that made me look up, but when I did, I couldn't see Harry. Maryssa and Jodie were still larking around, dashing in and out of the water and shrieking with laughter, but there was no sign of their friend. Concerned, I stood up.

'Jodie? Mo? Where's Harry?'

They stopped splashing each other and Jodie looked around too.

'I don't know, Mum. He was here just now.'

Then Mo splashed her again and the giggles resumed. My daughters clearly weren't worried about their missing friend.

I was, though. What on earth had happened to the child?

Then suddenly I saw a head bob up out of the water close to the middle of the lake. It was Harry. He opened his mouth, took a gasp of breath and disappeared beneath the surface again.

I don't think I've ever moved so fast in my life, either before or since. Kicking off my flip-flops, I charged into the water and ploughed my way to the centre. By the time I reached Harry, I could no longer touch the bottom. Doris was right. It was much deeper here. Grabbing Harry just as he surfaced again, I hauled him back to the point where I could stand straight and lifted him out. His little arms and legs clung on to me as he coughed up the water he'd swallowed, but apart from being frightened, he was otherwise unharmed. The gods were with me that day and I felt sick with relief.

Once I'd got him safely to the shore again, I wrapped him in a towel and held him tight.

'Harry, why didn't you shout, or call me?' I asked, frustrated and bemused at how he was apparently going to let himself drown without so much as a whimper.

'I d-d-don't know,' he muttered, his teeth chattering with the result of his shock.

'Were you afraid I'd be cross?' It was always a chance.

'N-n-no. I was s-s-scared,' he said, and promptly burst into tears.

I hugged him until he stopped crying and then we all got dressed and went home. Some sweet tea and biscuits later, he'd forgotten the whole incident and was playing with the girls in the garden again. I have to confess I never told his mother how I'd nearly lost her child; I was much too chicken for that. But then he didn't tell her

51

either. Perhaps he genuinely erased it from his mind or he was too embarrassed to admit he'd disobeyed me. Whatever the case, I was deeply ashamed for not keeping my eye more keenly on the ball – or in this case, on the child. I went into cold sweats just thinking what could have happened and continued to puzzle over why he hadn't made a sound as he prepared to drown.

Since then, though, I've learnt it's not uncommon for people to just give up like that. Cold water can numb the senses and the mind to the point where letting go of life comes all too easily. I didn't know it then, but I've never been more thankful about anything than I was for the intuition that made me look for him at that moment.

After the 'desperate drowning incident' as I called it, we nevertheless continued to swim in the Whites' pond, glad as we were to have a substitute for the dams that we used up on Cottingham Farm. The best thing about this pond was that it was shady and clean. The dams on the farm were used as water holes by the cattle and it wasn't unusual for us to be sharing our refreshing wallow with a few cows. They too enjoyed the cool water and would wade in up to their bellies. What they then slurped in at one end, they ejected at the other.

Strangely enough, I never thought or worried about the possible lack of hygiene; I simply appreciated the relaxed informality of our lifestyle. We were amused more than anything else, and since fish seemed to thrive in the dams, it can't have been that bad. But down at the Whites', I was quite glad to know we were the only ones likely to be polluting the water.

THE JOYS OF WORK AND THE SPOILS OF PLENTY

My job at Richmond Estates proved to be a blessing in a number of ways. For a start, I was grateful to have something to do other than staying at home now we were no longer on the farm. I missed the Ellenses terribly and I missed Bongi, Kheswa and their family too. On the farm, there was company and even though I had no job, there was always something to do. I wasn't allowed to work until our permanent residence permits came through, which only happened in 1984 shortly before we moved. It didn't bother me, though; when I wasn't doing the daily chores and looking after the girls, my time was my own. I used to occupy myself by making butter from the cream skimmed off our milk and soft cheese too. I made lemonade from the lemons on our bush as well as lemon curd, which one of my daughters still craves. I loved my life there and while I was proud of our little cottage in Byrne with its pretty garden and fruit trees, I felt a bit lonely without Ouma to talk to or Bongi to sit with on the grass, sharing jokes and games with the children.

With such a gap to fill, I was glad that once Lindiwe was installed to keep an eye on the girls, I could head into Richmond to act as secretary and administrator for Jean's 'boys', the four estate agents who worked there –

although calling what they did work is something of an overstatement. It was a retirement hobby for three of them and only John, the youngest of the four, could be said to be a working man. He was a farmer with land out on the road to Pietermaritzburg. He had a sunny-tempered and lively wife, Jane, and two young sons so in fact, he was the busiest of them all. With the calls on his time, I'm not quite sure why he felt the need to go into property sales, but he was the most serious about it.

The other three, Peter, Anthony and Gerald, were all retired and sold houses and farms as a part-time occupation – mainly to keep them out of their wives' hair, I would guess. From what I saw, they weren't very punctual and strolled into the office as and when they felt like it; most often it was just to pass some time before they strolled out again. The office was in an old colonial style building with a wide veranda on one corner of the crossroads in the middle of town. The other three corners housed a garage opposite, a liquor store diagonally across (locally known as a bottle store) and a bustling supermarket on the other corner. Our office shared the building with a haberdashery shop run by a well-conserved and smartly dressed forty-something woman whose name I've forgotten. All I remember is her stiffly permed helmet of brown hair that looked as if a hurricane wouldn't ruffle it and some rather forbidding black-rimmed glasses. She was very nice, though, and the shop was a treasure trove of wool, patterns, buttons and all manner of other sewing aids crammed into tightly packed shelves from floor to ceiling.

The 'boys' at Richmond Estates welcomed me warmly and were all very kind about my bungled attempts at typing. I'm sure they guessed soon enough that I threw away more sheets of paper than were ever sent out as letters. The typewriter was a golf ball electric machine, which would now be regarded as a museum piece. However, it seemed very modern to me then as I'd never used one before, so its snappy action took some getting used to. Bearing in mind I couldn't be called a typist by any stretch of the imagination, I was often in a sweat about how long it took me to bash out a single-paragraphed covering letter. If I managed to spell even the addresses correctly without three or four attempts, I would be jubilant. Unluckily for me, though, and I'm not sure why, but the usual self-correcting tape was not part of the deal. If I didn't want more Tippex (a white liquid we applied with a small brush) than ink on the page, I had to go very slowly and carefully. Still, I practised while the agents were out and eventually managed to type at a reasonable speed using at least three fingers and sometimes more. I remember John looking at me sideways once or twice as I crumpled yet another sheet of 'fine bond' paper into the bin, but he never said anything; nor did the others.

One thing I did know how to do was answer the phone properly, which was probably the more important skill since prospective buyers and sellers alike were mostly kept either waiting for a call-back or for the agents to finish with a client in the office. As Anthony and Gerald were often not there at all, I had to ooze soothing charm to the inevitably frustrated callers looking for them. In those days, there were no mobile phones and although I could ring any of the agents at their homes, I never gave their private numbers to clients. Asking anxious homebuyers to be patient was therefore an integral part of my job.

All the same, it was fun to work there and a very gentle toe in the door back into the employment world after spending the previous three years being a mum and farm girl. On a daily basis, I filled in sales contracts, wrote covering letters to lawyers, buyers and sellers, and maintained the petty cash, none of which was terribly demanding. If we made more than one sale in a week, it was cause for celebration. My professional tasks were regularly interspersed with making coffee and tea or generally talking to customers, many of whom just used to enjoy popping in for a bit of socialising. For all this weighty responsibility, I earned the princely sum of R375 a month, which would have been about $250 in today's money. Even then, it wasn't enough to live on, but it gave me some measure of independence – at least it did until things at home went financially pear-shaped. But that came later.

Of all of the 'boys', Peter was my favourite. He always had time to chat to me and he invariably sat himself down in the chair nearest the front door when he came in. Since this happened to be opposite my desk, it was a given that we would spend time putting the world to rights. Alternatively, he would entertain me with stories of his clients and sales. He revelled in gossip, so much of what he told me was related in a conspiratorial whisper and with a mischievous twinkle. With his shorts stretched over his round girth, his braces, knee-high socks, and red-apple cheeks, he bore more than a passing resemblance to Billy Bunter of literary renown. The only things missing to complete the picture were youth, which he couldn't have added, and a schoolboy hat, which he could have but didn't, preferring instead a battered and crumpled khaki cloth cap.

I don't remember meeting his wife, so perhaps he was a widower. What I knew for sure was that he had a wonderful garden with several avocado trees. When I happened to mention how much I liked them, he brought me two full carrier bags of the most enormous avocado pears I have ever seen. He planted them on my desk with a heavy thud and opened the bags to show me. I gawped at them, eyebrows through my hairline, mouth open wide. When I pulled myself together, I could only gasp.

'Peter, thank you so much! But we won't be able to eat all these before they go off. Surely there must be other people you can give them to as well!'

Peter wheezed and his body shook, which I knew meant he was laughing.

'Don't be daft, girl,' he said. 'Those are just a few of the windfalls. I could supply the whole of Richmond with what's actually on the trees. You take them and give some to your maid too.'

'But these can't be windfalls,' I replied, peering into the bags. 'They're perfect!'

'If you don't believe me, I'll take you to my place to see. I've got heaps of them.' He winked.

Of course, I was now embarrassed not only by the suggestion of my disbelief and my apparent ingratitude but by the uncomfortable awareness I should accept his generosity with a bit more grace than I was showing.

'Well, thank you again,' I spluttered. 'They're wonderful and we'll all love them, I know.'

'I'll bring you some fruit too,' he said by way of parting as he heaved himself to his feet and opened the door to the street. 'Cheers, m'dear!'

Sure enough a few days later, he arrived bearing more carrier bags, but this time full of plums. Oh dear. I'd forgotten to remind him we had two plum trees of our own, both loaded with fruit and attracting the region's entire population of wasps.

I managed to distribute the avocados quite easily as gifts. Even by South African standards, they were huge and received with suitable gratitude and awe. We ate a fair few of them ourselves but at some point, even those starved of such luxury can tire of guacamole salad, avocado dip and stuffed avocados when eaten every day. That day came quite quickly for us and it was a while before we could face including them in our menu again.

As for Peter's plums, they were instant overload. I took them home and without any guilt whatsoever handed them straight to Lindiwe, who already knew she was welcome to any of the fruit in our garden as well. I only hoped she managed to barter the excess for other things she needed.

As far as our own plums were concerned, it was a daily chore to pick up the over-ripe droppings. Since they were usually alive with wasps too, I warned the girls well away and forbade them to help me. We'd already had too much experience with stings when we lived on the farm. On that occasion, it was a swarm of bees that decided to take up residence under the girls' bedroom, and in fact Mo's first word was not 'mama' or even 'papa' but 'bee!', so I was a little paranoid to say the least. I didn't need to add wasp stings to the score.

With those I managed to pick before the mush stage, I made jam, jam and more jam. Then there were fruit mousses, plum and apple pies, plum juice and plum wine. And we were still at a loss what to do with them. It was so bad I became a kind of plum pimp as I'd positively solicit neighbours and friends to take them. The trouble was that most of them had their own trees, so we ended up shovelling them into a wheelbarrow and dumping them down on a heap at the bottom of the garden where they hummed with life until they were too rotten even for the wasps.

The other fruit trees in the garden were thankfully more moderate in their fecundity, but we had plenty of peaches, apples and oranges to add to our stores as well. The only thing I missed in our fruitful life was my lemon bush, and miss it I did. In some ways it was symbolic of everything I'd loved about living on the farm; it was the ultimate in exoticness and I equated it with our African life more even than the oranges that grew with such profusion in the valley. I never ever became blasé about walking out of the kitchen door and picking the lemons I needed for cooking and juicing. When I realised the cottage didn't have a bush, I was deeply disappointed and determined to plant one.

In most respects, however, the valley was much more tropical and African than the mountain. For a start, the summers were steamier owing to high humidity levels. Richmond was also very sultry and it was not unusual for me to arrive home from work at lunchtime and step straight into the bath to cool off. Tucked between the mountains, Byrne became like a sauna and for the first time in my life, I enjoyed the days when the mists came down. The drizzle soaked into the Kikuyu grass, turning the terracotta soil beneath it a mahogany brown. The resulting damp and chilly breezes were a welcome relief. On such days, we would go for long walks through the plantation that skirted Byrne Village, breathing in the aromatic scents of the conifers and enjoying the need to wear long sleeves, jeans and even jackets.

During these spells, I felt the valley and its surrounding ridges could have been Scotland. The scenery had an ethereal quality. The tips of the pine and blue gum trees disappeared into the clouds while trailing threads of mist hung over the impossibly green slopes. I could well imagine why the many immigrants of Scottish descent might feel at home there. The main difference was in the extent and variety of the produce. I very much doubt whether the Scottish highlands could have rivalled any of what I liked to call our spoils of plenty.

DOGMATIC AND CATASTROPHIC PETS

When we moved from the farm to Byrne, we just had our two cats, Mitten and Foggy, but it was inevitable that at some point we would want to have another dog. We'd had a gorgeous Doberman for a time the year before. Despite being highly trained, Cindy had failed the test for being a police dog, so she'd had to be re-homed. Apparently, she wasn't fearless enough. Bill heard about her from a client in what was then the Orange Free State and offered to take her. I felt then and still feel we were lucky to have been granted the privilege of having her and we loved her deeply. She was intensely loyal, wonderfully obedient and very gentle. My daughters could do anything they wanted with her and she made not a murmur of protest.

Still better as far as I was concerned, she adored me and protected me with a devotion that was comical at times. Even Bill could not come through the door without Cindy's permission, which was mostly not granted until I said so. She would stand at the entrance to the cottage as he approached and lift her lips, rumbling quietly. Being a Doberman, it must have looked ferocious although I doubt it was much more than a warning. Dogs are notoriously short-sighted, so it was possible she couldn't see exactly who was approaching until he, being Bill, came close, by which time I was there to greet him too.

When Cindy came to us, she was about eighteen months old. She died before she reached her third birthday. We'd been introduced early on to Redwater, a tick-borne disease that afflicted cattle. What we didn't know was that ticks could kill dogs too. At that time, tick fever was virtually unknown in Britain, so being new to Africa, we were unaware of the illness that South African dogs so often contract. Had we known, we might have saved her, but the early symptoms were not dramatic enough to spell danger.

Cindy suddenly went off her food one day and became lethargic. I thought she'd just eaten something nasty so didn't pay much attention until the second day when she was visibly worse. I mentioned it to Oupa Ellens; he looked at Cindy thoughtfully. I suspect he knew what was wrong but didn't want to alarm me.

On his advice, we took her to a vet in Boston, a village about ten kilometres from the farm. The surgery was in the vet's house, so it was more like taking Cindy to visit a friend, something that relieved me as I didn't want her to be frightened in her vulnerable state. The vet was a large, quite elderly man, but he picked Cindy up with ease and put her on the treatment table in his surgery.

'When did she go off her food?' he asked, feeling her over.

'Yesterday morning.'

'Hmm. Not good.'

Then taking a look at her gums, he sighed.

'She's got Billary, I'm afraid. I'll take her temperature, but see here,' he said pointing at her pale gums, 'this is a classic sign.'

'What's Billary? Is it dangerous?'

He looked at me over his black-framed specs.

'Put it this way, if you'd brought her in yesterday, I might have been optimistic, but I'm sorry to say it might well be too late.'

While I fought back the tears, he told us about the ticks, about the disease and how common it was. Most people kept the anti-Billary medication at home, he said. You could buy it at the agricultural cooperatives and if you even saw ticks on your dogs, or if they started looking off colour, it was normal to give them a jab. Nine times out of ten, this would prevent any further development of the illness. Tragically for us, this was all information we lacked. Ouma and Oupa Ellens hadn't thought to tell us; they might not have realised we didn't know about something so commonplace in South Africa. And for Cindy, it was definitely too late. Despite my efforts to see her through it by feeding her beaten egg yolk and minced liver with a spoon at regular intervals, she died a couple of days later as I sat beside her basket during the night. I was devastated.

The fact that there were three other dogs on the farm helped to ease the loss, but when we moved, the gap in the animal ranks was more marked. The day thus came that as a family, we took a drive to the SPCA (no R in the South African version) animal rescue centre in Pietermaritzburg to see if we could give a home to another unwanted hound.

I have to admit to mixed feelings about animal shelters. They're like hospitals. I know how much goodness there is in them, but they depress me no end. Seeing all the unwanted animals in cages tears at my heartstrings. I want to take them all home with me and give them the love they've been rudely deprived of. Making a choice of just one is agonising. Walking up and down the rows of the SPCA on that day remains indelibly printed on my memory. We passed cages full of small white Maltese Terriers, all yapping furiously, which was probably why they were there in the first place. We passed middle-sized dogs of mixed breed, many of which were painfully thin and mangy. Most of them wagged their tails on seeing us, their large eyes pleading and hopeful. I almost couldn't bear it. At the end of one of the rows, we came to a cage where a very large Dalmatian was sharing quarters with another large dog of indeterminate breed. While the other dog remained lying at the back of the small yard, the Dalmatian was nosing the chain-link fencing eagerly, straining to make contact with us. He showed particular friendliness towards the girls. Always a good sign. We wanted to be sure that any dog we adopted would be good with young children, especially as Cindy and the farm dogs had been so tolerant.

We looked at the details on the cage. The card told us that the Dalmatian's name was Brutus; that he was two years old (aren't they always?); that he was good with children and other animals. That was it. It sounded encouraging in any event. We decided to enquire about him at the office. After much debate, a test walk that revealed more about Brutus' enthusiasm for Bill than the latter's ability to cope with such a strong dog, and a lot of form filling, Brutus came home with us at the end of the afternoon. The only words of special advice we received were to be sure he knew who was the boss. I wasn't quite sure what this meant, but it didn't take long to find out.

Brutus was very large for a Dalmatian. He was muscular and well formed, albeit a bit grubby and unkempt. He'd been neutered, but maybe quite late in his two years, an age that I think was somewhat elastic in concept. My impression was of a mature dog in mid-life rather than a newly adult two-year-old, but who was I to argue? That said, he was everything the shelter claimed he was. He was marvellous with the girls, both protective and affectionate and as with Cindy, my daughters could do anything with him. He was also fine with the cats – our cats at any rate. I couldn't help noticing that anyone else's had him transformed from Dr Catkind to Mr Catskill in seconds. He would roar up to the fence, barking furiously, hair raised along the ridge on his back in an attitude of intense belligerence. I dreaded to think what would happen if he managed to get hold of one of the local feline population but hoped he was all bark and little, if no, bite.

Another problem that was more of an embarrassment than anything else was that Brutus was a racist. He would welcome white visitors to our house with tail wagging enthusiasm, but if any Africans so much as skirted our fence, he treated them to the same display of gnashing teeth and growling hostility that he did with strange cats. I later learned that most dogs were racist to some degree, but it worked both ways: if they belonged to European people, they barked furiously at African people, but if they belonged to the Africans, they were equally hostile to Europeans. I liked the justice in that.

Brutus did have one very endearing habit that I hadn't previously seen on a dog, although I know now it isn't unusual at all. He smiled when he was pleased to see us. He would put his head down a little, waggle his whole body from head to tail and grin goofily with his lips raised. It looked a bit like an evil leer, but we had no doubt he was trying to express his pleasure at seeing us.

In many respects, Brutus was a wonderful dog; the only snag was his attitude to me, which left something to be desired. Bill was the boss, no doubt about that, and Brutus respected him as such, but what was I? Brutus' demeanour to me was that of the favoured son to the master's skivvy, with me being the skivvy. I fed him, saw to his needs, gave him his jabs when I found ticks on him and walked him, but he totally refused to obey me. It was an ongoing argument that often ended with me walking away rather than obviously giving in. Still, with Bill in Johannesburg most of the time, I felt I at least had to be in charge, if not the boss, but Brutus had other ideas. When I found him with his nose in the sack of dry dog food, he challenged me with teeth bared. His greed was becoming legendary and I knew that unless I stopped him, he would eat the whole sack. The results would be explosive if not terminal. With guile and wile, I persuaded him away with a small dish of something irresistible – Bill's favourite sausage was the usual inducement, and while he was wolfing that down, I removed the sack to a higher spot in the utility room.

It was when I opened the door of my half-loaf van to go to work and he hopped in that the crunch came. Brutus loved going out in the car, which was fine with me, but not when he was sitting in the driving seat. The problem was he didn't agree that this was my place. This was going to be one battle of wills I had to win. I crossed my arms and adopted what I hoped was a 'take no nonsense' approach.

'Brutus, out!' I commanded firmly.

Brutus looked straight ahead and didn't even acknowledge me. He stared out through the windscreen with an expression that said 'If I can't see you, I can't hear you, so there.'

'Out!' I tried again, my voice rising.

This time he gave me a baleful stare, but still didn't budge.

'Look, you stubborn old goat, get off!' I yelled, giving him a shove.

He didn't move, but growled at me instead, raising his lips and showing all his teeth. In the general score keeping, it was a case of Brutus one, me nil. As usual. I was now feeling somewhat out-smarted, out-snarled and a bit desperate. I was also getting nervous. I needed to get to work and unless I could remove the spotted demon from the driving seat, I wasn't going anywhere.

In a last-ditch attempt to show him whose word was law even without his usual boss, I went inside to fetch his lead. I also grabbed a piece of chicken from the fridge. If I couldn't win honestly, I could always try bribery and corruption. I went back to the van where he was still sitting firmly behind the wheel. If it hadn't been so serious, it would have been hilarious, but I was in no mood for jokes. Waving the meat in front of his nose, I sneakily clipped his lead on his collar. As he grabbed the food, I yanked him out and slammed the door. That wasn't what he wanted though. After swallowing down the chicken, he turned on me and lunged at my hand, snarling angrily. I let go of the lead fast. Brutus swaggered back to the veranda trailing it behind him leaving me under no illusions as to who had really won the fight.

When Bill next came home, I told him what had

happened.

'I can't cope with Brutus,' I complained. 'He's too big, too strong and way too wilful for me.'

'Hmm. Perhaps we should get him a companion.'

'How do you think that will help?'

'I don't know that it will, but if there's two of them, maybe he won't be quite so dominant with you,' he reasoned. 'And if we get a female, that might work in your favour. He'll boss her around instead of you.'

'Okay,' I said, a little doubtfully and feeling more than a bit aware of my low position in the pecking order. 'It sort of makes sense, I suppose. Perhaps if he isn't the only dog, he won't be so inclined to challenge me.'

I'm not sure who we were trying to convince, but anyway, it resulted in the acquisition of a second Dalmatian, this time an adorable eight-week-old puppy. We called her Microdot. It seemed to suit both her and the circumstances given her very macro housemate. Later, Microdot was shortened to Microbe. An unfortunate twist, but somehow it couldn't be helped. Where she came from I no longer remember, but we fell in love with the adorable cartoon style puppy as soon as she arrived.

As with all young animals, she gambolled about, mostly being delightful, but not paying much attention to anything we tried to teach her. At first this didn't worry us much. In my admittedly limited experience of training young dogs, obedience schooling was nearly always a game to them and one in which they obeyed when it suited them or they wanted the reward they knew would be offered for good behaviour. But as time went on, Microdot's lack of response when we called her started to be of real concern.

By the time she was five months old, it was clear she was deaf. Even when I clapped my hands right next to her head, she didn't react. We took her to the vet's practice in Richmond. The vet confirmed what we already knew. Our puppy couldn't hear us even if she wanted to. The news we weren't prepared for was that there was nothing we could do about it. It seemed this was quite a common problem with Dalmatians and possibly due to the extent of inbreeding within a small 'family' of pedigree stock.

'Is there anything we can do to help her live a normal life?' I asked the vet.

'Not really. You can teach her things when she can see you and feel you, but that's about all. You'll have to keep her on a lead whenever you go out, of course.'

'Yes... of course.'

'To be honest, it might be kinder to have her put down.'

'No.'

'No? Are you sure?'

'Yes.'

Bill and I had agreed on this. We were far too fond of our bundle of spotty black and white nonsense to countenance putting her to sleep. How could it be kinder to have the life of such an affectionate, lively and cheerful member of our family snuffed out because she couldn't hear? She wasn't suffering; she knew nothing other than her soundless world. Apart from that she was perfectly healthy.

And so we learned to live with our deaf, but far from dumb, Microbe. Ironically, Brutus was indeed her saviour and mine too. Wherever he went, she followed; whatever he did, she did too. The only difference was that she loved me and he didn't, but that was okay. She certainly had a moderating effect on his behaviour if only because he saw himself as her guide. He was too busy being Microbe's hero to square up to me as much. Since Byrne Village was so rural too, it was easy to take them for walks along the forest pathways, soft with their carpet of moist needles, and then on the green slopes of the hillsides where they could run free without leads. Life for both dogs settled to a happy if unorthodox 'follow my leader' routine all the while we lived there.

As far as the cats were concerned, they continued with their core business of perpetuating their species by producing regular litters of kittens. Mitten, the queen of our menagerie, and the cat we'd had since our second year of life on the farm, always succeeded in getting herself pregnant again before she'd weaned her last lot of babies. I never managed to have her neutered in time. Foggy, our other cat, was half tabby, half wildcat. We'd found her on the road one very misty evening. The name seemed apt. She was a tiny scrap of a kitten herself when we brought her home, but even she ended up pregnant at some ridiculously early age.

Looking back, I think I might also have been very naïve about our farm cats' ability to procreate so frequently, but I honestly couldn't believe it when just a few months into our residence in Byrne, Foggy produced first one, then another and then another baby. I hadn't even noticed she was expecting. In the end, there were five of them, so where she'd been hiding them in her svelte form I was at a loss to imagine.

I'm inclined to think Foggy was part Civet cat or

something like that, as despite being very affectionate and sweet, she never lost her feral nature completely. When she had her kittens, she didn't want any of us to go near them. This was hard to explain to Mo, who was a mere three years old at the time. All she wanted was to play with or cuddle the adorable small sausages of mewling fur, but Foggy was having none of this. One day when I came home from work, I was met by my daughter in intense distress.

'Mummy, Mummy, the kittens have gone!'

'What do you mean? Gone? Gone where?'

'I don't know,' Mo sobbed. 'Foggy's eaten them. She's put them back in her tummy!'

'What? No, sweetie. She can't have done. That's impossible!'

I hoped I sounded convincing and I hoped even more it really was impossible. Where Mo got the idea from I don't know, but it was too awful to contemplate.

Nevertheless, we searched high and low for the kittens but couldn't find them anywhere. Foggy herself seemed completely unconcerned, returning to her normal behaviour and purring around us as usual. Whatever she'd done with her babies was clearly her decision, but I was certain one thing she hadn't done was eat them. They were already too big but even if so horrible a thing had happened, she would be looking very bloated. Apart from the usual saggy tummy and teats, she still appeared to be her usual size.

A few days later, though, I found them. Noticing Foggy going into the utility room and staring at the washing machine, I watched her in some puzzlement. What on earth was she doing? Then it dawned on me. With sinking heart, I opened the door of my precious front loader and there, in a soggy, humid heap were her kittens. How long they'd been shut in the machine, I didn't know. Normally we left the door ajar to avoid too much condensation, but someone must have closed it inadvertently. It could even have been me.

I lifted one of the sad limp forms out and checked to see if I could feel a heartbeat. There was. The kitten was still alive, if only just. I called Lindiwe to help me.

'Oh madam. Mo will be very happy now,' she said as she held a towel open to receive each of the kittens. They were hanging on to life by a thread, and I knew it would be touch and go.

'Lindiwe, we mustn't tell Mo. If she knows we've found them and then they die, she'll be very unhappy,' I said, stressing the 'un' part.

'Ha, yes, you are right. I say nothing.'

'Okay, then. That's good. What we're going to do is get them warm and dry, put them in a box in the shed and put Foggy there with them. I hope she'll feed them again, but if not, I'll feed them by hand.'

For the next hour, Lindiwe and I rubbed life back into the tiny bodies and before long, they were all squealing with hunger. After putting them in a box with some old towels, Foggy happily climbed in with them and started feeding them. This was a huge relief. Lindiwe and I grinned at each other and she then helped me to smuggle the little family into the shed. For the next couple of weeks, Foggy and her babies lived out of sight and in peace, but eventually, she brought them back into the house herself. She was finally ready to introduce them to the world. Fortunately, Mo was so glad Foggy hadn't eaten them and had 'found' them, we never had to explain our deception.

On the farm there were cattle, both cows and beef stock as well as horses. But there was no place for a cow in Byrne, not even a pony. Granted we had a big garden, but there wasn't enough room for anything of that size, so in a tongue-in-cheek effort to enhance the kids' animal education, we chose the obvious next best thing: rabbits.

Bill built a hutch to accommodate two bunnies in great comfort. There was a sizeable run with a small wooden kennel style hut at the end. Our idea was to move the combined unit around the garden providing the rabbits with fresh new grass every few days. The girls would then have the responsibility of feeding them dry food and giving them water. That was the theory anyhow.

One morning shortly after acquiring two delightful bundles of grey fluff, the ends of which were only distinguished by their long, silky ears, Jodie came running into the kitchen, her face crumpled with distress.

'Mummy, one of the bunnies has disappeared. I think it's Muppet!'

'Oh dear. Are you sure? Isn't she hiding in her house?'

'No, I've looked. I've looked everywhere and she's not there! And Mummy, the house is on its side. Kermit's still there, though.'

I couldn't help wondering how she knew which rabbit was which, and especially that the one which had gone missing was a 'she' because I certainly didn't know. At this point, though, it wasn't really the issue.

'On its side? Oh no! That doesn't sound good. Okay, sweetie. I'll come and look, shall I?'

She ran outside again and I followed, my heart sinking. I already had a feeling I knew what had happened.

Sure enough, the whole run had been pushed over and

was lying with its bottom open to any invader with evil intent. Mo was sitting next to it, nursing the remaining rabbit.

'Mo, sweetheart, take Kermit indoors and put him in a box in the bathroom for the moment. There's one in the kitchen cupboard. We'll sort him out in a minute, but keep him away from the cats and dogs.'

Tasked with such an appealing job, Mo scampered off clasping the little rabbit closely to her.

'Right, Jo,' I said, feigning command. 'Go and look in Father Muller's garden and see if you can see Muppet anywhere. Just be careful not to poke your hands into anything. You never know what might be there,' I finished, remembering our snake adventures.

Jodie nodded, climbed over the fence and set to work searching.

As soon as I had them both occupied, I went to find Brutus. He was lying on the patio at the back of the house. Down the front of his chest, there were large smears of blood.

'Oh boy. Look at you! You horrible dog! How on earth am I going to tell the girls you've killed their bunny?'

Brutus had the grace to put his head down between his paws.

I grabbed a bucket and cloth from the utility room, filled it with water from the outside tap and quickly washed the evidence from Brutus' face and chest. I thought I'd got away with it, but Jodie saw me from Father Muller's garden. The game was up.

Both girls reacted predictably. There were tears and tantrums and rages at Brutus, but in the end, peace was restored by the promise of another rabbit. When Bill came home on one of his increasingly rare weekends, he put a

74

mesh bottom on the run in an effort to prevent it happening again, but sadly, even this did not work; Brutus had developed a fondness for fresh rabbit. The second time, he managed to break the wooden hutch and in doing so, killed them both. At that point, we gave up. The stress for me and the distress for the girls were just too much. From then on, we just went to see the cows and chickens on the Whites' farm or when we visited Ouma and Oupa Ellens.

'Our rabbits weren't very African anyway,' I comforted the girls. 'What we'll do is look out for *dassies*. You know, those little furry creatures we sometimes see in the rock face beside the road? We'll try and watch out for them more, shall we?'

Since *dassies* are small African rock rodents, they look vaguely similar to rabbits and I thought this would be a good way of getting the girls to be more observant about wildlife. It worked for a while, but they eventually forgot about the loss of their pets and soon lost interest in *dassie* spotting in favour of Care Bears and My Little Pony. Being static toys, these creatures were easier to control, they didn't need feeding, and they could take them to their friends. Such is the fickleness of a child's loyalties.

CHRISTMAS IN BYRNE

Our first Christmas in Byrne was a memorable one, but not for the usual reasons. We'd already become used to reversing our seasons and in some ways, having winter in July was even stranger than having summer in December. Changing seasons required a mental shift that quite often had me confused as to what time of year it was, and even where I was. It wasn't a rare occurrence for me to lose track of the hemisphere we were in and to realise that because it was cold where we were in South Africa, that didn't mean it was the end of the year. I'd often have to spend quite some time unscrambling my brain and putting myself in the right location, month and season.

Likewise, having our summer holidays at Christmas was also odd although for the most part, we were used to it by the time we moved. Nearly all businesses closed for at least two weeks over Christmas and some, like the builders and plumbers, closed for the whole month of December. It was holiday time and the coast filled up with visitors from Johannesburg or the Orange Free State. Even so, it was Christmas and all the usual festivities had to be observed as well.

What struck me as amusing was the apparent need to keep to the European customary celebrations, or maybe it was more of an American influence. Despite being at least thirty degrees in the shade, most of the shops sported Christmas trees, jolly Santas and even fake snow in their festive season window displays. I remember feeling a bit bemused walking into the stores in 'Maritzburg during our first Christmas season. We could have been anywhere in Britain or northern Europe. We'd go from blistering heat outside into an icebox. The air-conditioning would be turned up to the maximum and the aisles festooned with tinsel, tree decorations and mounds of parcels liberally sprayed with silver aerosol paint. Christmas songs like 'Let it Snow' would be belting out over the speaker systems too. Incidentally, that particular song is always associated with Christmas but apparently it was written in a heat wave in Hollywood – just another of life's absurdities.

In any event, being in a South African department store in December was like being in a fantasy world, a kind of commercial Narnia. We walked through a door from Africa in summer into Europe in winter. The first time I experienced it I really couldn't understand that when most South Africans were gasping in sub-tropical heat and stripping down to shorts and singlets, they also wanted to perpetuate such an out of context celebration. But that's what they did and to a certain extent, it was what we did too. In the end I loved it. The almost bizarre juxtaposition of winter festivities with summer heat was perfect for someone like me who loved both the celebratory season and the sun.

Of the three Christmases we lived on the farm, two were spent at the beach in Port St John's and for the third, we combined Christmas and New Year by having a barbecue to celebrate both. We'd had all the decorations too, but now we were in Byrne at our own home, we felt a tree was even more important. I envisaged buying a small fake folding version that we could use again, but Bill had other ideas. Like many men of, shall we say, small stature he had a tendency to overcompensate. When he arrived home with our Christmas tree, it was not quite what I was expecting.

'Val, come and help me with the tree, will you?' he called from the garden.

'Okay,' I called back, wondering vaguely why he needed help, my mind still on that small, fake folding variety.

I went out of the front door and stopped. Bill's nifty company car was parked on the grass with what looked like a giant conifer sticking out of the boot. I wasn't far wrong. 'Giant' is maybe a slight exaggeration but the tree was a good three metres tall.

'Um, right,' I hesitated before continuing. 'Where are you thinking of putting that? Unless you're planning on raising the roof? Actually, no, forget I said that. We had enough roof-raising last year.'

I muttered this last part more to myself than to him, remembering how drunk he'd been at our barbecue on the farm. Bill was still living on stories of the 'leopard he nearly had a pee on' when he'd staggered off to relieve himself; a story that had its basis more in his fertile and alcohol-fuelled imagination than in truth.

'Don't be silly,' Bill huffed. 'I'm going to cut a piece off the bottom,' he said, and then after looking at it thoughtfully, 'and maybe off the top too. I got it cheap, anyway. I thought you'd like that.'

I decided to be wise and say nothing.

Between us we lifted the mammoth Christmas tree

(which was really a standard pine tree) out of the car.

After much sawing, measuring and cropping, we managed to leave half the tree in the garden, albeit in bits. The remaining streamlined version, custom-shaped to fit in one corner of the dining room, was eventually manhandled into a bucket filled with stones to keep it upright. It still touched the ceiling, so I stood on a chair and trimmed the last piece off. We had to have a fairy on it and we didn't want one with its head permanently bent over. It would have looked quizzical at best and, well, more than a bit sad. A sad Christmas fairy would never do.

Then came the decorations. The girls and I had enjoyed making our own on the farm. Now we had a really big tree, I was inspired to make even more. Matchboxes covered with Christmas paper done up with tiny ribbons hung next to painted pine cones and silver-sprayed twigs. We bought a string of lights, which the girls found suitably awesome having only seen them in shops before, and added some traditional coloured glass balls to the array. It was a truly beautiful tree and half the fun of that Christmas in Byrne was erecting it, decorating it and piling our brightly wrapped parcels under it. I forgave Bill for his excesses this time, especially as he really had got it cheap; for nothing, as it happened. It seems he saw it lying next to the road and decided it would save going to buy one, but he only told me this after we dismantled it in January.

All this activity was carried out in glorious hot weather with the dining room's French doors wide open. Visitors were welcome; we wore as little as was decently possible; and we took regular forays outside where I put trays of lemonade and long glasses for the children. Food was never something I followed the traditional line with so our Christmas fare was a mixture of *braai* (barbecue), salad, and mince pies. And, of course, plenty of South African beer and wine for the adults. We ate, drank and made merry, the women predictably sitting in one group while the men stood round the *braai*, talking rugby, cricket and cars and arguing about who made the best fire. The sun went down at its usual civilised time of around seven thirty in the evening and we were all in bed at our normal time. In short, a typical South African Christmas – until it wasn't.

I no longer remember on which of the Christmas holiday nights it happened but what I distinctly recall is that at some point during one of them, I woke up feeling cold. Not being at my brightest when I first open my eyes, I didn't register how strange it was to be so cold in midsummer. I must have just pulled the covers higher and gone back to sleep without thinking any more about it. What greeted our eyes in the morning came as a huge shock. The garden was covered in white. We thought it was snow at first but soon realised it was a thick coating of frost. We were flabbergasted. Frost? In December? In mid-summer? We'd never heard of it happening before, and indeed it was a rare and quite devastating occurrence. When we listened to the news, we heard just how bad it was.

'Last night a freak frost hit the Natal Midlands, the Drakensberg and large areas of the Orange Free State. Farmers are reporting extensive crop and fruit damage. This is the height of the South African growing season and losses will be severe.'

While for us it was a remarkable and memorable event, it was absolutely the worst thing that could happen to the farmers. I felt desperately sorry for them and many lost entire yields. It was also a reminder that we could never totally rely on the benevolence of the South African climate.

Nevertheless, by halfway through the morning any trace of the white blanket we'd awoken to had disappeared. It was a one-off weather happening and the rest of the holiday continued as normal with summer temperatures soaring to the mid-thirties, sometimes higher. From my perspective, basking in tropical heat was the ideal way to spend what in my English-born mind was a winter festival. I'd adapted with relish and never suffered from nostalgia over those cold winters of the past.

HEAT, COLD AND EXTREME COLDS

While I'm on the subject of temperature, summer was a steamy affair in the valley and I mean that without any innuendo. I know I've mentioned the heat before, but the humidity was such a change from living at the top of the mountain. Of course, we'd been through Byrne to Richmond many times before, so we'd encountered it prior to moving, but that was just for shopping, visiting friends or general trips into town and we didn't have to live with it. According to official information, our former home at Cottingham was over fifteen hundred metres above sea level, added to which it had a wonderful, fresh climate and air so pure and invigorating it almost sang. Byrne was four hundred metres lower and tucked into a valley. Meanwhile, Richmond and Pietermaritzburg were lower still, so the heat and corresponding humidity were even worse.

I well recall my first experiences of forty plus degrees; not that this was the norm but it wasn't rare either. On one occasion, we'd been shopping in 'Maritzburg and hadn't been able to find a parking space under cover. The temperature on that December day was forty-two degrees centigrade — in the shade. As we opened the car door, the heat blasted out like something from a furnace.

'Oh for heaven's sake,' I cried, shocked into

indignation by the inferno within. 'We can't sit in that!'

'We'll have to if you want to get home today,' Bill pointed out. 'It's not going to get any cooler till sunset.'

I tested the surface of the seats with justifiable trepidation.

'Ouch, ouch, ouch! That's dangerous, that is!' I complained as I almost parted company with the skin on my fingers.

'Just as well you tried it before you sat down in those shorts then, isn't it?' grinned Bill, ever sympathetic.

'These seats are a health hazard! They should come with a warning! Why on earth does anyone have vinyl seats in this climate anyway?' I snapped.

'They're not vinyl, they're leather... sort of.'

'No way! If they were real leather, they wouldn't get this hot!'

I knew I was grumbling, but it was with good reason. The car was in the full sun and we had what felt to be an interminable wait with the doors open before we could leave. To make matters worse, the steering wheel was so hot Bill couldn't touch that either. In my crabby state of mind, I couldn't help feeling there was some poetic justice there. Then to add insult to injury, Mo, who was still a baby, emphasised the pain by throwing up the juice she'd just drunk. Eventually, we managed to get going by spreading sheets of newspaper over the seats before sitting on them. This wasn't ideal as we all had newsprint on our shorts by the end of the trip. What the news was at the time, I don't remember, but it can't have been too scandalous; either that or we checked which pages we sat on first. Nonsense aside, it was the only thing we could find to prevent our backsides from being braised.

Anyhow, we were soon to learn that such soaring

temperatures were not unusual in the valley and when we moved to Byrne, this took some getting used to. Where on the farm I would arrive home and revel in the crispness of the mountain air, in Byrne I would peel my clothes off, slump into a chair and dream of air conditioning. It was a very sweaty business indeed and during the two summers we spent at the little house, the only times of day I really enjoyed were very early in the morning or after the sun had gone down. In between, we did our best to visit friends with swimming pools or those who had lots of shade on their verandas.

Alex and Bruce, our orange-farming friends, had a wonderfully shady property. Their land was a long strip that bordered the road and behind them rose the hills covered in conifers. Their house, which was not an old one, was a work-in-progress like the Whites'. It had a veranda all round and backed onto the trees. Since most of it was in the shade much of the time, it remained cool while we in our more exposed position in the village suffered the worst of the sun's ferocity. Near the trees, they had erected a large plastic paddling pool that they filled with a hosepipe. All the children loved splashing around in it and were just as happy there as they were in Doris White's pond or someone else's luxury pool. It was all water to them.

Sitting on Alex's veranda, I could look out over their large, informal garden and onto their orange groves beyond. Row upon row of small trees loaded with vivid golden fruit stretched for what appeared to be several hundred metres. I called them oranges, but I think they were really mandarin oranges or satsumas. In South Africa, they were called *naartjies*, a word that apparently derives from the Tamil word *nartei*, meaning citrus. I would guess the name was imported to South Africa with the early immigrants since it has been used in the country since the late 18th century. In any event, they thrived in the Byrne Valley, so I can only assume they liked the sub-tropical conditions.

'Is it always this hot down here in the summer?' I asked Alex one day. We were gasping like landed fish on her *stoep*, watching with more than a little jealousy as the kids splashed each other in the pool.

'*Ja*, well, *ja*,' she said, laughing. 'But I wouldn't complain too much. Better this than the cold in winter.'

'Well, it can't be any colder than it is up on the mountain.'

'Don't you believe it, Val. It's much, much colder down here,' she said. 'Just like the heat gets trapped in this valley, well so does the cold. You're going to wish you'd never moved from Cottingham by the time June comes around!'

And she was right. From the soaring forties of summer the temperatures dropped to well below freezing during the winter nights of June and July. It was cold overnight on the farm too and frost on the grass was not a rare occurrence but it always warmed up to a pleasant fifteen to twenty degrees by around ten o'clock.

In Byrne, the mercury plummeted below zero during the night, the grass was usually white with frost by daybreak, and it took much longer to warm the house up even though the maximum midday temperature outside was usually higher than up the mountain. But to make things worse, as soon as the sun disappeared over the top of the ridge around four o'clock, the cold galloped in again and before dark, we were already huddled in blankets on the sofa. Given that the cottage had no heating other than a small oil-filled radiator, we were rigid with cold much of the time.

I should mention here that the prevailing attitude in Natal was that winter only lasted 'a couple of months' (in reality, it's three) and since our stoic farming community maintained this short period could hardly be considered real winter, heating just wasn't necessary. The truth was, and this is no exaggeration, I have never been so cold anywhere as I was during the two winters we spent in Byrne and Richmond.

I'm not sure what 'real' winter was supposed to be. Maybe it was what they had in the Cape, as in wind, rain, snow and storms, but when I tried to complain about the cold to my South African friends, they used to look at me in astonishment.

'But Val! You used to live in England! Surely it's much worse than this!'

'Yes, but you don't understand,' I would say, teeth chattering. 'In England, we had central heating. It might have been colder overall, but at least we kept warm indoors. Here it's just as cold inside as out!'

'Oh well. It's only for a month or two, isn't it? And it's only at night, hey? Hardly worth the expense of central heating for that! Just wrap up warm, man!'

And that was always the answer.

Only Alex understood. She'd grown up somewhere closer to the equator and wasn't used to the cold at any time.

'You were right!' I told her one day. 'I wish we'd never moved!'

'Ach, never mind,' she replied, and I saw the

mischievous twinkle glint. 'It's only a couple of months of sheer hell. You can stand that, can't you?' I hurled an imaginary plate at her.

The way things went in the winter mornings was that after greeting Lindiwe who arrived swathed in a heavy poncho under which I could barely see anything of her except her well wrapped head, I would dress the girls and myself in thick sweaters, padded jackets, woolly hats, gloves and scarves before driving to Richmond. The little van barely had time to warm its oil up before we arrived, and the temperature gauge never crept above cold, so it was an icy cold ride into town.

When we came home at one thirty, though, it was as warm and sunny as an English summer's day. By then we'd stripped down to short sleeves, and the jerseys and jackets would be heaped up in the back of the van. Scarves, gloves and hats became quick casualties as they were easily forgotten or lost in the gradual process of shedding layers. Around mid-afternoon, we'd start putting things on again and by the time darkness fell, somewhere between five and five thirty in June and July, we all looked like Michelin men once more.

Even the cats and dogs were affected. Mitten and Foggy stayed inside, seeking out the best patches of sunlight to lie in and moving round the house with them. The two dogs shivered on the front veranda where they had their beds until I tucked them in at night with special grey felt blankets I bought from the trading store. I don't think they were intended for dogs, but I didn't ask and neither did they. They snuggled next to each other, sighing with contentment under the welcome extra layers.

The outcome of these fluctuations was not so good for

our health and this became apparent during that winter we spent in Byrne. It was icy in July so it was inevitable that colds and flu would abound. The first one to come down with severe flu was Bill. He was now accustomed to the Johannesburg climate, which being at high altitude was much the same as the farm's.

On one of his weekends home, he was already showing symptoms of a feverish cold when he arrived, but in Byrne's more extreme temperatures these rapidly became worse. By Monday, he was in a sorry state. The doctor pronounced pneumonia and prescribed bed rest and antibiotics. Bill, not to break the man mould, took to his bed with relish and indulged in the ultimate man flu: manumoania. And no, the spelling is not an accident. He moaned and groaned his way through several days of high fever during which I pandered to his every whim. I *did* actually feel sorry for him. At the end of the week he was on the mend, but that was when I started coughing. Within hours, I was by turns shivering and burning with fever so I too took to bed.

Unfortunately, this was not quite so convenient as Bill decided he was well enough to go back to work. He headed back to Johannesburg leaving me with the pneumonia he'd passed on, which by then had also developed into pleurisy. When I managed to crawl to the phone and call the doctor, she wanted to send an ambulance and have me hospitalised.

'I can't go into hospital,' I said, as firmly as my painful lungs would permit. 'I have two young children and no one to look after them.'

In the end, Doris White came to my rescue and took care of the girls for a few days while with the lonely help of antibiotics and cough medicine I sweated out the fever and the infection in my chest. I felt bad off-loading them onto her, but I'm quite sure all three of them enjoyed themselves and my small daughters were much better off with her than with me. I was about as much fun as a limp lettuce as I shivered under my piles of blankets.

What took me by surprise was that I'd always been a healthy soul on the whole and this was only the second time in my life I could remember being properly ill. It was quite a shock to realise I even *could* be that ill.

Nevertheless, I recovered, albeit slowly. It was only after I was fully back on my feet that I connected the illness with Byrne's climatic extremes and I promised myself I'd make sure we had better heating in the cottage before another winter came round. As things turned out, we only spent that one winter in Byrne, so the issue didn't arise again, but it was the one time in all my years in South Africa that I was sick of the climate.

THE SCHOOL RUN

In the 1980s, South African education was still segregated, so when I started taking my daughters to school, I experienced the reality of apartheid for the first time since I'd arrived in the country. Up on the mountain, we'd been removed from the legal iniquities of the government's race policies and although certain shops, such as liquor stores, still had separate entrances, we were rarely confronted with institutionalised discrimination in our rural world. In Richmond where largely speaking all the races patronised the same stores, we all mingled together; at least that's what it felt like. Unfortunately, when it came to education, there was no escaping apartheid. Even at the nursery school my daughters attended, all the little ones were white; black children were not allowed. This wasn't a matter of choice. It was a point of law, and it was a few years before we were to see any kind of integration in schools.

The local African kids went to their own schools and had their own uniforms. The poor teachers had to cope with much larger classes and the pupils had their lessons in much poorer conditions. We often saw them on the road walking to school, which said much for their determination. If they didn't manage to hitch a lift, many of them would have to walk several kilometres a day to get there and back. I hated knowing this and also knowing that my children received a better education if only because their classes were smaller and there was more opportunity for individual attention. The only way we more fortunate Europeans could help was to give lifts to the African boys and girls whenever possible.

Formal education in South Africa began (and still does) at the age of six. Until that age many of the local white children went to nursery or pre-school. The nursery school my girls attended was in one of the roads parallel to Shepstone Street, the main road through Richmond. Being so central it was easy to find and to reach. On the other hand and despite its location close to the centre of town, it was on a large and spacious property. The buildings were set on a big plot of land surrounded by tall trees giving the grounds welcome shade the whole day. The yard had the usual swings, slides and roundabouts necessary to a child's active happiness and a tall hedge at the front stopped errant toddlers from getting into the road. The playground always seemed to be full of dappled sunlight and was a lovely area for the infants to play in.

The school was run by a large, cheerful young woman who exuded kindness and caring. I don't remember her name now, but for the sake of giving her one, I'll call her Linda. There were other helpers there too, but Linda was the personality and the power behind the school. She was a born mother and great organiser and although (or maybe because) she had two children of her own, she had a fund of warmth to give the others in her care.

While the activities were mainly focused on interactive learning through play, the kids had some formal teaching in their last year of nursery, and many of them could already read and write by the time they started primary education or 'big school' as we called it. Both of my girls were avid readers and I was grateful for the help and encouragement the school gave.

At the end of the year, Linda always put on a Christmas show for the parents. I wouldn't have missed these events for anything. The performances were marvellous and very well put together with costumes sewn diligently by the mothers, myself included. But above all, they were priceless occasions for both pride and laughter, and usually had the audience spell-bound over the acting talents (or otherwise) of their offspring.

To add to the fun, there was always one child who danced to his or her own tune, completely oblivious to the one the rest of the children were following. Over the years these small individuals (bless them) were often the unwitting stars of the evening.

I remember one Christmas in particular when during the usual final nativity tableau, a very junior Joseph, who should have been standing serene and motionless next to Mary, started shifting uncomfortably from foot to foot. I held my breath wondering what was going to happen next. All the other young actors were taking up position, singing sweetly out of tune and looking suitably holy when suddenly, Joseph clutched his crotch through his robe, stared in wide-eyed panic at the audience and announced 'I need to pee!' To gales of laughter from the assembled parents – except perhaps his own – Joseph rushed off stage, leaving his poor five-year-old Mary gaping and the donkey giggling helplessly behind her.

After the Christmas show, there would be a graduation ceremony for all the children who were leaving to go to proper school. It was hopelessly twee, but also very touching to see them in their mini black gowns and mortar board hats, clutching the scrolled-up leaving certificates they were presented with. It was the sort of occasion that would strike most sensible souls as pretentious and ridiculous, but I'd defy any parent not to feel a rush of warmth and pride at seeing their babies all dressed up as miniature scholars. It was the ultimate in cuteness.

Both Jodie and Mo loved their time at nursery school and made friends with many other kids in Richmond, a development that meant my life after work changed substantially as my half-loaf van became 'Mom's Taxi.' It wasn't unusual for me to have a van full of chattering tots in the back that I shepherded from one house to the next. And they all loved travelling with me in my ultra small minibus. There was only one downside to all the kid-carting and that was the constant squabbling that used to go on when I took the girls to and from Richmond. I suppose nearly all siblings bicker; it's how they negotiate their relationships with each other. But Jodie and Mo never let up, particularly in the van, and it drove me to distraction. I threatened to turf them out a dozen times. On one occasion, I did.

I'd turned off the tar road and was driving up the graded dirt section towards Byrne, a stretch of about ten kilometres that ran between plantations of tall pine trees. In the back, the girls were arguing intensely about nothing as usual.

'You've got my hair band!' Yes, it could be that banal.

'No, I haven't. You've got mine!'

It's not!'

'T'is!'

S'not!'

This was then followed by a howl of indignation.

'You pinched me!'

'Didn't touch you!'

'You did!'

'Didn't!'

I roared.

'Shut. Up. Both of you!'

Of course they didn't so my temper, usually slow to arouse but this time sorely tested, flipped. I stopped the van at the side of the road.

'Enough! I'm sick of your fighting. I want you both out. You can walk home. I'm going!'

'No, Mummy! You can't!'

'Yes I can. Now. Out you go!'

I climbed down from the van, pulled back the sliding door and stared at them with thunder in my face until they both sheepishly got out and stood by the roadside. I pulled the door closed, got back in and drove off leaving them standing there. I didn't go very far; I never meant to. The minute I pulled away, the tears began. I watched in my rearview mirror as the two little mites stood in the muddy ruts at the side of the road, holding hands and sobbing. I suppose I'd gone about a hundred metres before I stopped, put the van into reverse and drove back to pick them up. They were so shocked I'd actually done what I'd threatened to do so many times before, they didn't say another word until we got home. The peace and the truce must have lasted at least a week before it all started up again.

The time then came for Jodie to go on to Richmond Primary School. She turned six in July 1985, so by the following January, when the school year began, she was one of the older starters. Richmond school served a wide catchment area being a farming district, and because of the distances, many of the farmers' children were weekly boarders. It seemed tough to me to see so many six-year-olds being left at the boarding house on Sunday night every week. Remembering how much I'd hated boarding school myself, I was relieved I didn't have to leave my own child to the care of others.

It also occurred to me that even if they had to spend hours travelling each way, at least the African children were able to go home to their large, noisy, embracing families every day. There were no boarding facilities for them so they were spared the wrench of that weekly parting. But perhaps I was projecting my own dislike of boarding on the situation. Maybe they would have preferred to stay at school rather than endure the exhausting trek every day.

The primary school's buildings were typical of those in the region. They were brick-built and consisted of long single-storey structures constructed in a u-shape, rather like stables – only in this case no animals other than the two-legged variety were involved, except perhaps the occasional class rabbit. There was a covered veranda that ran the length of the inner side of the 'u', onto which the classroom doors opened. This meant that if it was raining, the children wouldn't get wet as they proceeded from lesson to lesson. It also helped to keep the classrooms cooler in the summer. But in winter, the school was freezing. There was no heating and the doors were mostly left open. What made it worse for the children were the school rules about uniforms, which I found totally nonsensical.

Firstly, wearing the correct uniform for the season was compulsory regardless of the vagaries of the climate. Officially, summer began on the twenty-first of September so whatever the weather at the time, the girls had to wear a thin gingham summer dress in blue and white check and short white socks. For the boys, this was grey shorts and a short-sleeved shirt. There was a school blazer and they also had cardigans, but they weren't allowed to wear the blazer over the cardigan. It was one or the other. It also didn't matter if it was cold, wet and nasty during September, which was often the case in spring. On the day of the spring solstice summer uniform had to be worn whether we parents liked it or not.

Likewise, when the twenty-first of March came round, all the children had to switch to winter uniform, which for the girls meant long-sleeved white blouses and navy pinafores, school ties, school jerseys and knee-high socks. The strange rule about the blazer not being worn with the jersey still applied. Again, the weather usually didn't cooperate with this decision on the part of the school authorities.

March is autumn in South Africa, and in Kwa-Zulu Natal, it is generally hot and dry, the summer rains having usually dried up earlier in the month. The poor children practically expired with heat until the mornings became cooler in April and May and only really cold in June. Most of July was the winter holiday so when the schools started back in August, it was beginning to warm up again before the changeable spring season struck in September again. The winter uniform was only truly practical for about two months of each year but as often happens in these bureaucratic environments, practicality and rules were at odds with each other.

I have never been good at following regulations for their own sake. If I can't see a valid reason for a particular directive, the rebel in me wakes up. When Jodie came home complaining about being too cold in her summer uniform, I sent her off the next day in long socks and a jersey beneath her blazer without demur. When she was hauled over the coals for wearing the wrong clothes, I wrote notes of complaint on her behalf. The same happened in winter. I just couldn't understand the logic of being so rigid about the day on which the changeover took place. It would have made much more sense to postpone it at least a month to October and April, but sense had nothing to do with it.

As far as I knew, I was just one voice so I suppose the school administrators were as fed up with me as I was with them. As things transpired, this kind of ongoing conflict over what I deemed to be petty rules was a pattern that continued throughout both girls' South African education until they finished their studies. I never learned. But then neither did the schools.

In Richmond, one of the standard annual problems was head lice. Every parent dreaded the moment when the call came from the headmaster's secretary. When Jodie had been at school for about six months, it was my turn.

'Hello, is that Valerie, Jodie's mum?'

'Yes, speaking.'

'It's Richmond Primary here. I'm afraid we'll have to ask you to come and fetch Jodie. We've had an inspection today and we've found lice on several of the children.

Jodie has them too. She'll have to stay home until you've managed to get rid of them all.'

'Oh lord. Yes of course. I'll come right away.' This was one rule I couldn't flout,

As I dashed off to the school, I started scratching my scalp. It's amazing what auto suggestion can do.

The school secretary received me in her office with a very shame-faced looking Jodie.

'I've been trying to tell your daughter there's nothing to be embarrassed about. Lice are not a sign of dirty hair. Quite the reverse, in fact. The doctors tell us that they're actually more attracted to clean hair.' She winked at me, a conspiratorial gesture that had me wondering whose leg was being pulled: mine or Jodie's.

In any event, once one child had picked up nits, as we called them, they swept through the school and no matter how carefully we washed and brushed our children's hair, it was inevitable that they would have them at least once during their school life. Since Jodie's hair was thick and waist-length, it was even more inevitable that she would get them.

There was only one solution and that was to cut her hair short, which we did with much ceremony and, for me, sorrow. She had beautiful dark, wavy tresses that positively rippled down her back. It almost hurt to chop them all off. Luckily, Jodie was excited to have a new, easy, cropped hairstyle. What she didn't like so much was the somewhat vicious shampoo we had to use to kill the lice.

'It burns!' she cried. 'Ow, Mummy, take it off, please, please!'

'I can't, Jojo. I'm sorry. It has to stay on for at least five minutes or it won't work.'

'But it hurts!' she wailed.

'Darling, you want to go back to school, don't you?'

'Yes. I suppose so.'

'And you don't want Mo or me to get nits, do you?'

'No.' Sniff.

'Then just wait a bit longer and I'll be able to rinse it off. If it's worked, we won't have to use it again, but if we don't give it long enough, we might have to.'

That thought was enough to make her bear it, despite the tears dripping off the end of her chin. It was heart breaking. I consoled myself with the thought that several other parents were going through the same painful rigmarole.

Then came the daily combing with a special, fine-toothed nit comb. It reminded me of searching for fleas on the cats; the lice were much harder to see, though. When I thought I'd really got rid of them all, we went back to school for an inspection. Jodie and I were both as nervous as a couple of exam candidates being put to the test.

The school secretary greeted us again.

'Oh how pretty you look with your short hair now, Jodie,' she smiled. She knew all the right things to say.

But when she took her magnifying glass and comb to what we thought was Jodie's squeaky clean scalp, she frowned.

'No. I'm sorry. She can't come back yet. There are still a few lice in her hair. They're probably dead, but she can't come back till they're all gone.

Oh dear. Jodie's face crumpled. Back home we went.

'Never mind, lovey. Just see it as a few extra days of holiday,' I said, trying to lighten her mood.

'But I'm so bored at home now, specially when Mo's at

school and you're at work.'

'Yes, I know, but Lindiwe's very kind, isn't she?'

'Yes.' Sniff.

'And you've got lots of books and drawing things.'

'Yes.' Sniff.

'And it'll just be a few more days.

'Okay.' Sniff.

And it was. Just for certainty, I subjected my poor child to one more treatment with the 'burning shampoo'. She endured it bravely, convinced now that this was the only way she would be released from the worst of all fates: the tedium of staying at home. A few days later, she was given the pass to go back to school. It was like being told she'd won an award.

On another later occasion, Mo too got lice from school and we had to go through the same process all over again. It was one of the more common risks of African life although not restricted to farming areas. There were head lice scares even when we later moved to Johannesburg and the girls were at school there, but as far as I recall neither of them got nits again. Forewarned is always forearmed and we learned to check for them regularly. It was an occupational hazard but more so while we were living in an area where so many children spent their lives doing what is otherwise the best thing for them: playing outside in a completely natural environment.

The standard of education set at the primary school was high. Classes were structured, discipline was strictly maintained without – I think – being cruel and the children had homework to do every day, even from their first year. What this achieved was a strong level of self-containment in the pupils, and from that time on, Jodie never had to be told to do her work. Nevertheless, it's true that these days, the punishments they received for bad behaviour would be considered unacceptable. It was not unusual for girls to be rapped over the knuckles with a ruler and for boys to be caned. Since I too had this kind of discipline at school, I didn't feel it was anything to complain about at the time especially as they only got the stick when they'd been properly bad.

Other misdemeanours usually just resulted in detention and Jodie was no stranger to having to stay after school to write lines or do some other punishment task. She wasn't a naughty child; rather the opposite, but she had an unfortunate tendency to get caught doing things wrong in, dare I say, slightly naïve attempts to cover up mistakes or accidents.

There was the memorable time in her first school year when she'd been swimming and hadn't allowed enough time to get dry and dressed before going back to class, so she'd just pulled her school dress over her swimsuit. In temperatures of thirty degrees and over, the drying time was rapid and the risk of telltale damp patches minimal.

The problem was, the wearing of school uniform over swimwear was not allowed – yet another of those rules. So when the changing rooms were inspected, there was an unclaimed pair of underpants left lying there, these being my daughter's. In her haste, she'd forgotten to pick them up and hide them in her school bag. As I said, she was a bit naïve. If she'd intended to be disobedient, she'd have made sure she didn't get caught. I like to think so, anyway.

That being said, the consequences couldn't be avoided. The offending navy knickers were produced in class and held up for all to see.

'Whose underpants are these?' enquired her class teacher with studied calm.

No one answered. Nor did Jodie.

'Right then, we'll have to find out the hard way then, won't we?'

All the girls had to line up and lift their skirts to reveal what they had, or didn't have, underneath. My poor child's fate was quickly decided. Apart from the embarrassment of being exposed in front of all her other class mates, she then had to stay behind and write a hundred or so lines confirming her underhand (or was it underpants?) sins and promising not to commit them again. I have a feeling she remembers this incident far more than the odd rap over the knuckles, although I don't think either did her any lasting harm.

RICHMOND

Although we lived in Byrne, the fact that I was working in Richmond and both girls were at school there meant it increasingly became the centre of our world. My first impression of Richmond when we arrived in 1981 was of a colourful but shabby mess. I was seeing it with English eyes, and I remember being shocked that it had been described in the guidebooks as a 'charming village' representative of the old colonial style in its architecture. To me it looked anything but charming, used as I was to the quaint stone and thatch cottages with their flower filled gardens of my former English home in Dorset. Peeling paint, corrugated iron roofs and rickety verandas didn't strike me as being all that appealing.

Later on, when I realised quaint and cute was not what it was about in my new country, I started to see through the sun-bleached decrepitude and appreciate the buildings for their gracious proportions. I came to love the delicate tracery of the wrought-iron work on the shady verandas as well as the patchy curved sheets of rusting tin on the roofs. These old houses had an integral elegance very much in keeping with their surroundings. Richmond Estates was in such a building and inside, the ceilings were high with beautiful mouldings and decorative cornices. But there was still no denying the shabbiness on the streets.

Pavements were uneven with broken stones. In many places they had subsided, and the cracks between were filled with dust, scrubby grass and litter. The kerbs were high to accommodate deep storm water drains, for when the heavens opened, as they often did on summer afternoons, the deluge of water needed somewhere to go. Fast. The rain came down in stair rods, the sheer weight of the water enough to soak us in seconds. Within half an hour of such a downpour, the streets would be dry again, or if not, steaming gently in the intense heat. But without the high capacity drains, the risk of flooding would have been real.

At other times, there would be heavy hail showers that would leave cars pitted with small dents. This was more hazardous as hail was often local and unpredicted. On more than one occasion, I drove straight into a wall of icy bullets and had to stop to wait it out. Trying to drive on a road covered in hail was similar to trying to walk over a carpet of ball-bearings. Uncontrolled would be putting it mildly.

The weather conditions could consequently be harsh on all types of structures, but especially on the tarred surface of the road. It was so degraded from the battering it took from the heat and precipitation, it looked like patchwork where the potholes had been filled in, and war damage where they hadn't. The whole effect was that Richmond was a town in need of repair. All the same, I grew fond of it for its vibrant mix of faded charm, clattering noise, and rich smells.

Richmond is on the main route from Pietermaritzburg to Ixopo and thereafter to the Transkei, so Shepstone Street, being the through road, was cut by just one major intersection. Chilley Road crossed it at the four-way stop on the corner of which was the only garage and petrol station. At that time, it was already a Caltex garage and still is if Google's Street View is to be believed. By the time we moved to Byrne in 1984, I was quite used to the amazing service we received there (and at most other garages too), but I never quite got over the feeling of being unduly pampered when I pulled in to fill up my tank. It was so unlike anything I'd ever experienced in Europe and as far as I know, things have not changed even today.

What happened was that as soon as I pulled in, two or sometimes three young men in company overalls would rush out to serve me. They used to positively bounce with energy and nearly always wore wide, cheerful smiles. Being a fuel pump attendant was a much prized job, mainly because of the generous tips they received; hence the bright and shiny customer service.

'Fill it up, Mama?' the first one to reach my open window would ask.

'Please!'

'Oil and water? Tyres? Windscreen?' he would prompt, the hope gleaming in his eyes. The more they did, the higher the tips. Of course.

'Just the oil and water today, thanks Daniel!' Or Moses, or maybe Amos. They usually wore name badges, so we could address them by name. It made it so much more personal.

'Yes, Mama. You give me key for petrol cap please?'

I would duly hand over my keys, and then pull the bonnet lever. I should also mention here that 'mama' or 'auntie' seemed to be standard forms of address, which I quite liked. They were a nice mix of courtesy and what I took to be real friendliness. At least I hope that's what it was.

Anyway, while Daniel filled up, Moses or Amos (or whoever was part of the team) would check the oil and water and one of the three would wash my windscreen whether I wanted it or not. I enjoyed watching them do this; it was such a well-practiced routine.

They would bring a bucket of soapy water over with a sponge, a window cleaning squeegee and some paper towels that they used to keep the rubber wiper part dry. The windscreen would first be liberally soaped with the sponge, and then with quick, skilful pulls, the dirty water would be wiped off on first one side and then the other. Lastly, the ever-present cloth they kept in their pockets would be whipped out to clean off the last drips and polish the screen to spotless perfection.

They delivered all these services with the fluid agility of a choreographed performance and I couldn't help but smile. They well deserved their tips even if they did things I hadn't asked them to do. I confess I always felt very spoilt and missed the friendly banter of the garage guys when I later returned to Europe and the much blander do-it-yourself method.

On the garage side of the crossroads, Chilley Road led off into a quiet residential area; on the other, it sloped gradually down hill until it reached the edge of a plantation. This part of Chilley Road was home to rows of small African and Indian stores, most of which were in old settler homes that only appeared to remain standing by leaning against each other somewhat precariously.

Chunks of plaster had fallen from their facades, and the true colour of their once vivid paintwork was masked by a layer of reddish dust. The cracked footpath in front of many of the shops was kept shaded by tin roofing supported on rusty iron or brick columns. Despite its apparent flimsiness, this cover provided shelter against heat and rain for the goods the proprietors heaped outside. There were boxes of knobbly root vegetables, gem squash, butternuts and turnips. Then there were crates of huge, over-ripe tomatoes, creamy maize cobs known as 'mealies', sacks of sugar, flour and maize meal (the staple food stuff of most of the locals).

In between the grocery shops, there were clothing stores and shoe shops that also fought for space in the shade. With all these goods on display, there was no room for customers, so the shoppers walked in the road or sat on the curb on the other side of the street in the full sun. There they would gather in throngs, talking at the tops of their voices in order to be heard over the hooting of horns from frustrated drivers, especially on paydays.

To drive down the hill to the large, airy supermarket at the bottom was a challenge that had to be met with patience, a gift most people didn't have; hence the horns. Much of the time, I walked there from work if I didn't have too much to carry. It was infinitely quicker that way even if it meant having to jostle my way through groups of women whose slumbering babies were strapped to their backs in shawls. How the infants managed to sleep so deeply with all the cacophony around them I will never know, but it probably meant they were inured early in life to all the noise in their family huts at home. I have to say I never saw a Zulu baby crying or in need of a dummy to keep it quiet.

Adding to their small human bundles, the women often carried large items on their heads; these could be anything from a sack of potatoes to a mattress. They looked magnificent as they proudly bore aloft what sometimes seemed to be half their home and I was constantly amazed at the grace and dignity of their posture and movement. But it meant that as I negotiated my way through the crowds, I had to watch out for obstacles both overhead and underfoot.

It was a mad mêlée and while it could be frustrating at times, it was mostly fun to feel part of such a vibrant throng. Interestingly, we never worried about pick-pocketing as we ploughed our way through press of people. I'm not sure if it's just not done in Africa, or maybe I was just lucky, but in all my twenty years in the country I never had anything stolen from my bag or person. If I put something down and turned my back on it, it would be gone in a flash, even a pair of glasses, but I never experienced any of the light-fingered pocket theft that goes on so much in Europe.

The supermarket at the bottom of the hill was part of the Spar chain of stores that seem to be as ubiquitous as Coca Cola outlets. Like most food shops in South Africa at the time, it had that faint smell of meat that has passed its sell-by date. I don't think it was necessarily because the meat was bad; more likely it was because the supermarket stocked all the parts – some might say 'delicacies' – that African people enjoy so much. These included bags of chicken's feet, beaks and claws, chicken livers and all sorts of other ripe and smelly offal. I used to make a point of avoiding the big freezers where all these rather graphic reminders of what the animals used to be were stored. That aside, it sold more imported goods than any of the other shops and stocked good cheeses, cold meats and fresh vegetables, so I went there on a weekly basis.

One of the other pleasures of shopping at a South African supermarket was the help we received with filling our bags. In England, I'd mostly had to scrabble around trying to fill up my carrier bags as fast as the checkout girls totalled up the prices of the goods. I hardly ever managed to keep up and mostly ended up loading my things back in my trolley so that I could pack my bags in peace away from the till. In South Africa, there was always a helper, and not only that, the bags (which were pretty flimsy affairs) came free, so it didn't seem to matter how many they used. There was a girl to ring up the goods and another one to pack the bags and they were as quick as each other, deft and dexterous as they were. It was fun to watch them even though I felt a bit useless. Added to that, they were usually friendly, which made shopping a much more bearable experience. And this went for every supermarket, not just our local Spar.

Our regular bulk buying was done at the Indian owned supermarket just down from the four-way stop on the way out to Byrne. I mentioned in my previous book that it was called Bridgeway Stores or maybe it was Bridgeway Supermarket. Whichever it was, the shop was a cross between a rural trading store and a normal supermarket. It had all the sacks of meal, flour and sugar that the rural traders sold as well as a huge variety of other tinned convenience foods and household goods.

Bridgeway sold electrical appliances, plastic buckets, bedding, clothing, cosmetics and even LP records. Everything was cut price so it was there that I used to buy Lindiwe the skin lightening cream that all the Zulu girls used along with my own lotions and toiletries; all much cheaper than at the Spar or the pharmacy.

Despite its obvious economic appeal, shopping at

Bridgeway was an exercise in fortitude for someone like me. I can deal with crowds out in the open where there is plenty of air, but in the confines of narrow shopping aisles, I become quite seriously claustrophobic. Bridgeway's aisles were very narrow owing to the goods not only stacked on shelves that reached almost to the ceiling, but also heaped up on the floor and in every possible nook and cranny. It was a real test of my endurance to weave, squeeze or (as was often the case) shove my way through the hordes of shoppers. In Europe, we tend to have quite a strong sense of personal space. In Africa, this is less so. A lot less so. There were times when the press of zealous customers around me had me in a state of near panic.

As for the noise, it was deafening. I found it fascinating that the Zulus, who were used to living at such close quarters with each other, felt the need to speak as if everyone in their immediate vicinity was deaf. It was mystifying. Not that their voices were unpleasant. Not at all. I just didn't understand the need for nothing less than maximum volume.

Maybe it had to do with the way they communicated across wide valleys and distant hills, which they did with wonderful and breathtaking resonance. But I couldn't help wondering why they couldn't turn it down a notch or two for more intimate settings, especially when they were less than a metre apart.

All the same, I loved Bridgeway as much as I loathed it. It was such a treasure trove of wonderful stuff. Like a condensed form of a French hypermarket (or maybe I should say compressed), you could find pretty much anything you needed if you were prepared to hunt for it: from sewing materials and fabrics to gardening tools and gas bottles. It was like having all my favourite shops in one and at half the price. But my greatest and most thrilling find of all was in the records I found stacked up in a vegetable rack at the front of the store.

In our early days in South Africa, there were no CDs or downloads. The only form of music we had was in the form of cassette tapes. Our battery-operated radio at the farm had a cassette player, which made them (the tapes) the obvious choice. We couldn't play vinyl records without the electricity to turn the turntable and on the farm there was no electricity at all. To compensate, we would often spend evenings sitting in Bill's company car with the doors open, listening to music. It was the only stereo player we had then, but it was quite magical to be outside and gaze up at the unbelievably brilliant banner of stars while we hummed along to our favourite songs.

When we moved to Byrne, we owned a grand total of three cassettes: Janis Ian's Night Rains, Juluka's Scatterlings of Africa and the Moody Blues' Long Distance Voyager. With the arrival of the little half-loaf bus, I was happy to find it also had a good stereo and we could drive along with our music at full blast. There was nothing guaranteed to lift the spirits more than hurtling along a dirt road leaving a dust trail worthy of a spaghetti western, and feeling the heat blasting through the windows as we bellowed along with Johnny Clegg, Janis Ian or Justin Hayward.

I never considered the implications of the triple Js back then, but maybe the telling part was that after a time, I for one wanted more variety; after all, the alphabet had another twenty five letters, didn't it? So when I noticed Bridgeway Supermarket had LPs for sale, I couldn't resist flipping through them from time to time. No matter that we didn't have a record player yet. The albums were fifty cents each and even in the 80s, that was absurdly cheap. It was worth buying a few and finding a turntable later.

When on one occasion I was about halfway through the pile, I found several albums by a Zulu group going by the name of Ladysmith Black Mambazo. I'd never heard of them before, but in some kind of flash of premonition, I felt they might be important. I bought two of their records and took them home but as we hadn't yet indulged in any kind of sound system they weren't much use to us.

In the end I packaged them up and sent them to my sister, unaware that within a few years, the band would be rocketed to fame as the supporting musicians in Paul Simon's Graceland album. I would imagine those two pieces of vinyl are collectors' items now and I'm often tickled by the memory of buying them from the stack of cheap records piled above the onions at Bridgeway.

Sometime later we *did* manage to acquire a record player and we started collecting a few LPs. As well as the Bridgeway collections, I used to haunt local jumble sales around Richmond in the hopes I'd find some more bargains. One other fifty-cent special I came across at Richmond Primary School's annual fair was possibly one of the best discoveries I have ever made. I was walking round the sports-field-turned-fair-ground in the hot sunshine, idly looking at the usual array of white elephant stalls, home baked goods and bric-a-brac. It was at one of the last that I saw a box full of records on the ground beneath the table.

'Anything good in there, Pam?' I asked the mother of one of the girls' friends who was manning the stall.

'Yes, actually. They were ours, so I can vouch for their

condition too,' she replied with a grin.

'So why are you getting rid of them?'

'Oh, you know. When you hear things too often, you get tired of them.'

By now I was thumbing through the LPs but stopped when she said this. I was looking at the cover of Jeff Wayne's War of the Worlds. It was a musical I'd only ever heard parts of on the radio, but I knew it was brilliant.

'You got tired of this?' I held it up for Pam to see, incredulous that anyone would want to dispose of it at a school fête.

'Ah yes, well... yes, we did,' she laughed. 'To be honest, I never liked it much in the first place. Do you want it?'

'Do I ever! How much?'

'Fifty cents and it's yours.'

'Deal!'

I snatched it up, barely believing my luck. It was a double album and in perfect condition as Pam had testified. Within days, it became a family favourite. Jodie and Mo were spellbound by both the music and the story, the latter being narrated largely by Richard Burton whose legendary voice added much to the record's hypnotic attraction. The girls would sit cross-legged on the floor next to the turntable as if they could see the whole story in that revolving piece of plastic. Since we had no television in Byrne, this music was the next best thing to a movie and I was rather pleased to know I'd scored such fantastic and rare finds not once, but twice, in Richmond.

ENTERTAINING OURSELVES ELSEWHERE

During the months that followed our 'winter of discontent' when we'd been so ill, the already noticeable cracks in Bill's and my relationship widened into a cavernous gap into which a glamorous and sophisticated woman more suited to his corporate ambitions easily slipped. There's an old saying that 'two's company, three's a crowd' and this was one of those situations. To cut the sorry story short, Bill moved out and we agreed to put the cottage on the market.

Initially, it changed little in the way the girls and I lived in Byrne. Bill's home visits had been increasingly rare and we were already used to him not being there. The main difference was that we started spending much more time away at the weekends. Since we had more freedom to do what we wanted with our free time, we took to going visiting more instead of staying at home.

Unfortunately, I'd lost touch with some of the people we knew from the other side of the mountain as we no longer went to the Elandskop tennis club. In our first years, we'd spent most Saturday afternoons at the club, which had a small library in the backmost of the back rooms. We rarely played tennis, Bill having disgraced us both early on by upsetting the club protocols and refusing to take seriously his responsibility as match organiser of the week. We were henceforth ejected from the tennis teams, much to our and everyone else's collective relief. Instead, we browsed among the surprisingly well-stocked shelves and took home piles of books each week. We read voraciously in those days despite having no electricity and having to squint at our print by the light of oil lamps and candles.

The other benefit of the tennis club was the social aspect. We'd made some good friends in the Elandskop area, but as often happens, we stopped seeing them after we moved further away. Even worse, we hardly even saw Ouma and Oupa Ellens when we started living in Byrne and this was something I wanted to change. Shortly before we left the farm, Ouma had been in hospital with breast cancer and she'd had a mastectomy. She was fine the last time I saw her, but I wanted to be sure she was still doing well.

Phoning people in rural areas was always a challenge. The farms still operated largely on a party-line system with old-fashioned phones that had handles on the side. They had no dials or buttons and to call a neighbour or the exchange, the handle had to be turned to make it ring; the more you turned it, the longer the ring. Each home on the line had its own number, and I remember the Ellenses' was 1722. Their code was one short, two long and two more short rings. It was complicated to say the least and frequently resulted in confusion. As a result, when I wanted to call Ouma from a normal phone, I had to ring the Elandskop exchange and be put through by the operator, but it wasn't rare for the wrong person to pick up. A call might therefore go something like this:

'Good morning. Is that Elandskop Exchange?'
'Yes, dear, who would you like to speak to?'

'Paulien Ellens, please.'

'Hold on, I'll try the number.'

There would then be a series of beeps of alternating length, a bit like Morse code.

'Hello, Margaret Evans speaking.'

'Sorry, Margaret, I was phoning Paulien.'

'Oh, I'm so sorry. I thought that was our code. Actually, I don't think Paulien's in.'

'Isn't she? Okay, well if you'll just put down, I'll try again to make sure.'

'I will, but before I go, can I book an overseas call please?'

'Margaret, I've got a caller holding on for Paulien. I'll call you back afterwards, Okay?'

'Okay, but you won't forget will you?'

'Margaret!' There followed a pregnant, meaningful pause. 'Just put the phone down. I'll get back to you. I promise.'

Margaret would oblige at last, and then we would have to start again.

I eventually gave up phoning; it took too long and was too frustrating. It seemed much easier to head up the mountain to go and see them in person, so this was what we did.

With the advent of spring and the rainy season, we took the opportunity only when it wasn't wet. For all its advantages, the half-loaf was no Citroen and was not equipped for dealing with muddy mountain roads. We needed a dry day for this particular visit. The first time we went, I realised with some guilt it had been several months since I'd ventured up to Cottingham. It was a sunny, warm spring day and as we climbed up out of the valley, my heart lifted. The incredible beauty of the scenery never ceased to make me catch my breath. I remembered that when I first saw it I knew I would never live in such a breathtaking environment again and the memory of its grandeur remains with me still. When we reached the final rise at the top, I would slow down or even stop to gaze out at the panorama ahead of me. Fold upon fold of hills stretched away into the distance to culminate in the craggy ridges of the Drakensberg Mountains.

Early in the spring, the berg, as we called it, still had snow on its peaks. The view spread out, presenting itself to us like a gift as if to say 'Look your fill. Stretch your eyes as far as you can see.' As we reached the crest of the ridge, I cut the engine. There wasn't a sound other than the whisper of the wind in the grass, the faint creak of an old windmill and the rattle of its rusty blades whirring round. The freshly green slopes were scored by *dongas,* deep cracks that had formed through erosion; the bare hills were peppered with dark shrubs and the occasional thorn tree. And then there was that singing air. And the steely blue sky. I felt a wonderful sense of aloneness that was both exhilarating and inspiring.

A hawk swooped and hung a moment, hovering above the ground until suddenly, it dropped.

'Mummy. Why have we stopped?' chirped a voice from the back.

'I want to see Ouma,' chimed in the other.

'Can we go now? Can we, can we?'

'Girls, look at this wonderful view. Did you see that hawk? Oh and there's a Secretary bird. Look!' I pointed to the striking red-eyed, white and black bird, striding through the grass on its long legs.

'Yes, but Mummy, we want to see Ouma.'

117

I sighed and started the engine again. My daughters had grown up with this – here, on the farm. For them it was normal. It was only for me that it was all still so amazing. In this situation I was the child full of awe and they were the bored, jaded grown-ups who'd seen it all before. How come they had already lost their sense of wonder? Or maybe I'd been the same at their age about London and its great buildings. I consoled myself with thinking they'd appreciate it later. I hoped so, anyway.

We coasted down the sand road, past a small dam, up another rise and then turned in through the old familiar five-bar gate. It felt odd to be just visiting; not to be coming home here. Danny and Suzie, the Ellenses' large and bouncy dogs came roaring down the steps of the veranda to greet us as usual, but this time, we wouldn't be driving round the side of the house and parking in front of the annex. It wasn't our home anymore. Another couple lived there now and I felt a pang of jealousy.

Ouma came out onto the veranda to greet us. Despite the stick on which she leaned for support, she looked just the same and was, as always, wreathed in smiles.

'Hello, hello,' she called, laughing. Jodie and Mo ran to her and were both gathered into her ample arms for a big grandmotherly hug.

As she straightened, she pulled at her dress and briskly shifted her bosom into place. Seeing my expression, she laughed again.

'Ach, Val, you know this birdseed boob I wear is always slipping out of shape.'

'Birdseed? You *are* joking aren't you?'

'*Nee, nee.* It's true,' she chuckled. 'I hated the falsie they gave me at the hospital. Such an uncomfortable *dingus*.' Her own special Dutchlish word for a thing. 'So I made

118

my own from birdseed and muslin. It needs some improvements though.' She looked down at its uneven, lumpy shape with a frown.

'Well, you'd better not let it get wet,' I said, laughing.

'*Waarom niet, hé?* Why not?' She asked, forgetting I wasn't Willem, her husband, and slipping into her native Dutch.

'Because if you do, it'll start sprouting shoots and then it'll be an even funnier shape,' I told her.

Ouma laughed till she cried, and I did too, which made the girls curl up with giggles as well. Seeing her like this made me remember again how much I'd missed her.

Following her round to the side of their lovely old, single storey, colonial style home, I saw that Oupa Willem's work-in-progress was still there. He'd been building a sailing catamaran ever since I'd been in the country, and it still looked some way from being finished, propped as it was on trestles and covered with a large tarpaulin.

'How's the yacht going, Ouma?'

'Ach, *ja*,' she pouted, waving at it dismissively. 'I don't know. I don't ask. It keeps him busy though, that and the vegetables.'

She looked over to the vegetable garden on the far side of the paddock facing us. Beyond the two cows grazing next to the fence, we could see Oupa's bald head bobbing up and down. He was bending to pick the day's crop from the neat mini-dykes he always dug in the large vegetable patch. I was convinced this was his way of maintaining at least some of his Dutch origins. Jodie saw him too and ran over the grass to greet him. She adored her Oupa and although she had too much to think about now to miss him, she was excited to see him again. A few minutes later, she was holding his hand and skipping along beside him as they made their way up to the house.

We spent a precious couple of hours with them, the only uncomfortable note being when we met the new tenants of our old home. They were a middle-aged, hippie-style couple who clearly felt it was their duty to look after their elderly landlords and seemed a little possessive to me. Still, Ouma and Oupa valued them and didn't appear to feel suffocated so I had to assume they didn't mind. Maybe they even liked the coddling as a new development.

Other things had changed too. Bongi, the maid they'd had while we were on the farm, was no longer with them. She'd been an angel with my small daughters. She must have been about nineteen, but Ouma told me she'd met a man, got married and moved to Pietermaritzburg. She'd left for good not long before. Later on, I heard she'd wasted no time in producing her own babies and ended up with four children.

The Ellenses now had Mahwile, Bongi's stepmother, working for them and she remained with them until they moved from the farm. Mahwile was everything Bongi was not. She was small, wiry and strong in contrast to Bongi's bulky frame, and she'd survived giving birth to fourteen children. Where Bongi had been noisy, confident and jolly, Mahwile was quiet and softly spoken. But I liked her. She was kind and thoughtful and gave me the impression of being a rock on which Ouma could depend.

The other member of the household of whom I was very fond was Kheswa, the Ellenses' farm hand and Mahwile's husband. He was both sinewy and wily and had a mischievous sense of humour. It was his doing that

I'd learnt to milk a cow when we lived there, mainly because he occasionally fancied a day's 'sick leave'. We didn't see him this time, but I hoped we'd see him again. Apparently, he was getting old and didn't do as much as he used to, another development, and this one saddened me. He'd been fit and lively when we left less than a year ago.

Once we'd made the first move, we went to visit the Ellenses several more times, and it was on one of these occasions that I heard something that was going to bring about the greatest change of all. The farms along the side of the mountain and in the valley below were to be incorporated into Kwa-Zulu, the areas designated for the Zulu people. It was part of the process that was happening all over the country. Apartheid was gradually being dismantled and in Natal, land was being re-allocated. The intention was supposedly to improve the lot of the Zulu population and give them more space under their own government.

'We've all got to go, Val,' Paulien told me. She was smiling but I could see the sorrow in her eyes.

'But what will happen to Kheswa and Mahwile, and the family? They'll all lose their jobs, won't they?'

'Yes, that's the worst part. Willem and I will be fine. We'll move to Howick. We're getting too old to live up here, anyway, but it's going to be hard for them.'

'All for the greater good, I suppose,' I said, and in principle, that was true, but I never knew what happened to Mahwile, Kheswa and their children once the transfer went through. They were all employed on the farm, so how they were going to survive, I didn't know.

It was inevitable that all the farmers, farm workers and tenants in the Elandskop area would have to leave; they would have no choice. It was a government decision and compulsory. Whether they received much in the way of compensation or not, I don't know. It wasn't something we discussed, but in 1987 when I left Natal to move north, everyone on the mountain had gone. When I saw Bill and Paulien Ellens a few years later, they were settled in Howick, a town north-west of Pietermaritzburg.

Another outing I enjoyed was going to the book exchange in Pietermaritzburg. There may have been a library in Richmond, but I don't remember going there. Book exchanges, on the other hand, were a huge attraction. The idea was to keep swapping books you'd read with other books in the shop. They were all second-hand and for every book the customers took in, they would receive a credit note. The amount was dependent on the book's condition.

They could then select more books from the shelves. These were priced a little higher, so although they always had to pay something, it wasn't very much and the customers were helping to keep the exchange stocked. It was also possible to go in and buy books without having any to hand in, but it was much better to do a trade-in.

The one I went to was crammed with paperbacks and the aisles were much too narrow, but it was an absorbing place to waste a few hours and then retire to a café for coffee and a browse through my purchases. In those days I was a great action adventure fan and I would look for authors like Wilbur Smith, Dick Francis and Hammond Innes. I also loved Jack Higgins, Alistair Maclean and best of all, Desmond Bagley whose books were serialised on South Africa's wonderful radio station, Springbok Radio.

South Africa was subject to sanctions when it came to music and live performances, but books still seemed to be freely available and book exchanges were thriving businesses. Armed with enough reading material for a month or so, I would drive happily home feeling I'd had a great day out.

Closer to the village, and in fact just round the corner, was the Oaks Hotel, or the Oaks at Byrne as it is now known. These days it's quite an upmarket and smart establishment with luxury accommodation on stunning grounds and, predictably, lovely oak trees. In the 80s, as I remember, it was just a relaxed, rather informal country guest house in an old building with a long deep veranda on which there was a random collection of comfortable chairs and sofas. It was also about the only place to go for a drink close to home. Now and then a few of us such as Alex and Bruce and another couple, Anita and Phil, who lived on the edge of the village, would go and sit in the shaded comfort of the hotel's veranda and chat with other customers over a beer and a glass of wine.

As usual and by unspoken agreement, the men and women separated and gravitated towards their single-sex groups where they could conduct conversations on their particular favourite topic of the moment. After more than four years in South Africa, I was used to the ways such social conventions operated, but I never quite understood it. I'd given up asking for explanations a long time ago. It was just how it was and any suggestion that we women might want to mix with the men was received with blank, puzzled incomprehension.

Visits to the Oaks were a luxury I couldn't afford all

too often but it made a pleasant change on occasions. It should be said that good wine was so cheap in South Africa we could easily buy a box of five litres for somewhere around R5 (about £2.50 at the time) and drink much more for much less around the *braai* in our own gardens, but going to the Oaks was such a treat.

There wasn't much else to do in Byrne and Richmond but we loved our rural life. We visited neighbours like the Whites and the girls' school friends who lived on the farms in the area. One of these families, the Connells, rented a house on a huge property and they had horses, so riding was occasionally something we could all enjoy, something I've loved it since childhood despite being a bit nervous of horses. In fact, I even looked after other people's in England. Then when we lived at Cottingham, we used to ride the farm ponies regularly, usually without saddles and always without hats. It was risky and I was often unseated (a polite way of saying what I really did, which was just to slide off) but it was one of those pursuits I felt was worth the fear for the fun.

At the Connells, we'd go out hacking with Richie, the father, and his two daughters. They were much more experienced than I was but because Jodie and Mo liked to ride as well, I could make an excuse for taking it slowly. Jodie would sit behind Richie, or one of the older girls, and Mo would be with me. Together, we roamed over their farm. It was heaven.

I thought there could be nothing more exhilarating than cantering leisurely along the tops of the ridges with the sun on my back, the wind in my face and the horizon stretching away ahead of us. The majestic peaks of the Drakensberg marked the skyline whichever direction we took. They changed colour and definition with the light and were breathtaking in their shifting moods.

Other than these rare adventures, we were invited to *braais* and birthday parties, and every so often we joined a group of local friends at Midmar Dam or its bigger brother, Albert Falls Dam, the two huge reservoirs that supply water to the Natal Midlands. Both dams allowed boating and swimming, a welcome bonus for us especially as we could reach either of them for a day out. We'd load up the car with blankets, food and utensils, not to mention dogs, kids and ourselves, and drive the seventy odd kilometres to Midmar or ninety to Albert Falls.

The scenery on route was magnificent. The Midlands' area is all hills, with steeply undulating grassland and smooth green pastures. From Byrne we had to drive across country on mainly dirt roads and the lonely splendour of the rolling hills made my heart swell every time. I suppose in many ways, the scenery is similar to the dales of England's Yorkshire and the Peak District of Derbyshire. In South Africa, there are just fewer roads and even fewer houses.

That said, the weather in Natal is much more stable than anywhere in England, which is one of its more notable attractions. It was easy to plan an outing and be relatively sure we wouldn't be rained off. It was also a lovely drive to either of the dams and a trip I never found a chore.

As soon as we arrived, we'd set up camp under the trees where we would have our picnics. If someone had brought an inflatable boat as well, we'd all pile in and go hurtling round the dam at great speed. Occasionally, someone else might bring water skis and I liked to watch, guessing how long it would take for those souls brave enough to try it to fall off.

'Why don't you give it a go, Val? You look as if you'd love it!' Alex once asked me as she waded out of the water having taken a number of dives off the skis.

'Me? You must be kidding!'

'Why ever not? I thought you loved speeding around in the boat.'

'Ah. Yes, well, that's because I'm in it, not behind it or, knowing my luck, under it,' I said, repeating a mantra that has been a constant throughout my life.

'But it's fantastic! Really.'

'I'm sure you're right, Alex, but there is only one thing I dislike more than being cold, and that's being wet and cold. That water is freezing out there. I'd die of hypothermia...and don't tell me not to exaggerate.' I finished, raising a warning finger.

'So I take it that's a definite no,' she said, grinning.

'Yes,' I laughed.

These day trips to the dams were marvellous and the girls loved them. They charged in and out of the shallows, playing with their friends and the dogs. It did me good to see them enjoying the sun and water so much. The only problem was keeping enough sun-block on them. Every time they went in to swim, they washed it all off, and Jodie nearly always came home with a burnt nose. I used to worry that she'd do some permanent damage to her skin, but as she grew older, there was thankfully no sign of scarring.

The great benefit of almost everything we did for entertainment when we lived in Byrne was that it involved being outside. Despite the long and cold winter nights, Natal's climate was ideal for leading an outdoor existence. As long as I could afford the petrol, we could entertain ourselves simply by enjoying our surroundings in good company.

And then, there were our weekend trips to the coast.

BEACH TIME ADVENTURES

Because my job at Richmond Estates didn't pay very much and support from Bill wasn't always forthcoming when I needed it, we couldn't afford to go away to the places we'd been used to going when we lived on the farm. There were no more trips to Port St John's on the Wild Coast; no excursions to the Drakensberg; no beach holidays on the north coast. It was too expensive to travel so far and then to find accommodation for the girls and me. But it didn't matter that much because we found a different kind of adventure that we enjoyed just as much; well, nearly, anyway.

The Ellenses had a daughter, Helen in Durban. She and her husband, Tom, had become good friends over the years and they invited us to stay with them.

'Come on down, Val. You know we've got plenty of room and we'd love to see you. The boys will be over the moon too.'

They had two sons, Johnny and Tim, who were just a fraction older than my two, but they all got on well and played happily together. For me, Helen's company was immensely cheering. She was warm, fun and practical. Now I look back, I can see she also had many of her mother's qualities, one of which was what I now recognise as her inherent Dutch good sense. She was just as unfazed by life's twists and turns as Ouma.

'Are you sure you don't mind us all descending on you, Helen? The thing is I can't leave the dogs alone.'

'Dogs, kids, cats, who cares? Bring them all,' she said breezily.

In the end we didn't take the dogs, much as I hated leaving them behind, especially Microbe who was so much my dog. It would have been too much – for me, not her. Each time we went, I arranged for one of the neighbours to look in on them and feed them, but Helen wouldn't have minded having them there. I'm sure of that.

She and Tom had a fine, sprawling house in Westville, a suburb on the hilly outskirts of Durban. It was an older home with high ceilings, large rooms and plenty of light, despite having huge trees in the garden. They both worked from home and in fact, it was at their house on one of our early visits that I saw my very first fax machine.

I am easily awe-inspired and such a piece of wondrous technology struck me as symbolic of South Africa's advanced telecommunications. For me, the memory of seeing it is bound to South Africa because it impressed me so much. Even more, I was convinced Tom and Helen were the most modern business people I'd ever met. The fax was an impressive piece of equipment and they proudly showed it off to me. I was astonished when I saw what it could do and Tom's demonstration was worthy of a salesman's pitch.

'Look at this,' he said drawing an outline of his hand on a piece of paper.

'Very nice, but what are you going to do with it now?' I

asked, slightly puzzled.

'Well, the machine will scan this image when I feed it through this slot here.'

'What's a scan?'

'Ah, yes, hmm. Let me think.' Tom scratched his chin. 'I think you could say a scanner is a device that reads images. You'll notice that tube thingy that the paper passes across, ok? Well that's what scans the picture or text.'

'Yes, and then what?'

'It takes a precise reading of whatever's on the paper and converts it to information called a bitmap. A bitmap can be sent through the telephone lines to produce an exact facsimile of the original – hence the name fax – to a receiver anywhere in the world.'

He was losing me in all the 'technospeak'.

'Um, does the receiver have to have a fax machine too?'

'Yes. Watch. I'm going to send this one to someone in England. But first I'll put a message on it and ask them to send it back.'

'Why would you do that?' I asked, still bemused.

'So you can see what it can do, dummy,' he said, smiling.

Five minutes later, I was stupefied to see Tom's drawing coming out of his fax machine, not only with his hand written message on it, but with another one from his friend as well. Talk about seeing magic for the first time.

It's strange now to think that these machines that became essential office equipment during the eighties and nineties are now largely redundant. I remember they got smaller and smaller and eventually were no bigger than a flat A4 sized box with a phone receiver on one side. Years later we had them at the medical aid company I worked for in Johannesburg, but after the arrival of the internet, photocopiers and mobile phones, no one seemed to use them much anymore. All that amazing technology has almost disappeared and the only place I see fax machines these days is in the heaps of redundant old office machinery at jumble sales or in junk shops. It's quite sad really.

Anyhow, Tom and Helen's home became a kind of refuge and escape for me during the stressful months after Bill's departure while I waited for the house to be sold. Whenever it was possible, we would head down there for the weekend. I used to fetch Jodie from school on Friday and with the little van packed with our own provisions, we'd make our way towards the forever-holiday-feeling of Durban's coastal climate.

The route was through Pietermaritzburg and down the N3 from Johannesburg, which was a good road all the way to the coast. Most of it was dual carriageway even in those days. The highway swept down through the province with spectacular views of the Valley of a Thousand Hills to the north.

This famous area with its fairytale, almost Tolkeinian scenery and hillside villages was real Zululand. It had a mystical beauty that always made me think of the settings for those legends and stories that are passed down from generation to generation in the Zulu culture; it was landscape that evoked tales of mystery and magic and much of it was still remote and quite inaccessible.

The route to Durban was, and still is, known for another more active reason. Every year, thousands of impossibly sporty types run almost ninety kilometres from Durban to 'Maritzburg (or vice versa) as participants in the Comrades Marathon, one of the great ultra marathons and perhaps one of the toughest. They don't run on the highway (at least I hope not; there'd be more being run over than running) but the course follows parallel roads, which could even be more gruelling, gradient wise. To this day, I find it impressive and take my hat off to the runners, walkers and even disabled people who take on the challenge, bonkers though I personally think they must all be.

Nevertheless, it's such an inspiring day in the South African calendar and brings back fond memories for me of the great Bruce Fordyce, who won the Comrades nine times between 1981 and 1990. He was credited with putting the concept of 'comrade' back in the marathon when he wore a black armband during his first winning run in 1981. Apparently, it was his protest against the 20th anniversary celebrations of the apartheid regime.

I think we were all a little in love with Bruce Fordyce then. He had rather romantic looks and for me it helped that he and I were born in the same year. It felt like some kind of connection, ridiculous though that might now seem. There's no reasoning with hero worship, is there?

The first few times we went down to Durban, we stayed at Helen's home, but as time went on, we branched out and spent a few weekends at the beach where Tom, Helen and the boys would join us in their own camper. Later still, we went on our own, but that was only after we'd moved to Richmond.

Camping on the beach was a special experience. I'd missed the trips to Port St John's on the Transkei Wild Coast where we'd stayed at the municipal campsite right next to the most beautiful of beaches imaginable. Parking between the bushes that edged the sands down beyond

Amanzimtoti and towards Kingsborough on the Natal south coast was the next best thing.

The little van could just tuck into the gaps in the vegetation without going onto the beach. Even the low coastal evergreen trees with their twisted limbs managed to provide us with enough shade to keep the van from roasting in the midday heat. Tom and Helen parked as close to us as they could and we formed a small encampment on the rough grassy patches under the coral trees and bushes.

Natal's south coast beaches are ideal for families with young children. There is endless sand, plenty of shallow water and intermittent rock pools. Ours did what all young things loved: they built castles in the sand, buried each other with unwholesome glee and jumped in and out of the waves. But best of all, they loved peering at the tiny fish and flies darting around in the pools trapped by the layered slabs of rock. It kept all of us, me included entertained for hours as we clambered from one stack of rocks to the next.

In the evenings, we grilled sausages on the *braai* for the children, who ate them between rolls of crusty white bread filled with salad. We adults ate much the same, but with more salad and chicken or chops instead of sausages. The smell of smoke from the charcoal hung in the evening air and to this day, the whiff of a barbecue reminds me of the heat and salty air of the South African coast.

As the light faded, rarely later than seven thirty in the evenings, we drank wine from a box, chatted and laughed and only reined the children in when they became too boisterous. These were good times and they did much to distract me from the growing stress of my situation at home.

We arranged it so the children all slept in the half-loaf. I could fold the back seats up so both the boys and the girls could lie like sardines in a row in their thin cotton sleeping bags, their sun-drenched skin needing no further covering. I had a bunk in the camper with Tom and Helen. It was a perfect arrangement. All four children had a ball but hardly any sleep because they giggled half the night. We could hear them larking about because we left the sliding door ajar on one side of the half loaf and the windows open, confident that it was perfectly safe.

On that note, we were beginning to hear murmurings of trouble around this time, but as far as we knew it was not widespread. Up until 1985, we'd led a charmed life. It never occurred to me that we needed to watch out for our possessions, lock our doors and secure our windows. We didn't have burglar bars or security systems and any ideas that our personal safety was at risk never entered our heads. I might be wrong, but it was as if we were enjoying the calm before the storm.

Apartheid was being slowly broken apart and we'd seen changes to the pass laws, as well as some relaxation of the segregation laws and many other iniquitous practices already. However, it wasn't enough and we all knew it. The coloured, Indian and black people still had no political franchise and tensions were rising, not only between the government and the people, but between the different factions within Zululand. All the same, during those marvellous sunshine filled weekends at the beach, none of these rumblings reached us. We were two families finding simple enjoyment in making do with what our surroundings offered us.

In the morning, the sun would be high and the

campers like ovens, which had us all out of bed early. Long walks along the never-ending sands culminated in eating a leisurely lunch, cleaning up and packing the vans before heading back. For Tom and Helen, this just meant home to Westville. For the girls and me, it was a longer drive back to Byrne, quite often a slow one too. Many South Africans from the inland towns of Pinetown, Hillcrest and Kloof would also be at the coast at the weekend, so the roads could be busy.

If I really wanted to avoid the traffic, I could take the 'back road' from Kingsborough to Richmond. It was narrow, winding and full of potholes, but it was sometimes quicker – unless we got caught behind an old truck struggling up the hills, belching diesel smoke and lurching drunkenly over the road. It was a gamble that sometimes paid off and often didn't, but it was a beautiful route through the semi-tropical landscape of the coastal sugar cane fields and banana plantations, and then up into the impossibly green hills of the Midlands.

The most noticeable difference between our visits to the Natal coast and the earlier times when we'd been to beach in the Transkei was that at the latter, there was no racial segregation at all. The Transkei was one of the Bantu homelands and there we met the African children on the sands too. Oddly, we rarely saw their parents, but my daughters played with local children and it was on our first trip to the Wild Coast some time in the winter of 1983 that we met a young Xhosa boy of unusual grace and calm dignity. His name was Sobriety and we spent some especially memorable time in his company.

In Natal, it would be the end of 1989 before the beaches were officially de-segregated by order of President F W de Klerk, still another four years to go.

That said, much unofficial integration had already been going on for some time before the pronouncement was made. But when we went to the south coast beaches in the summer of 1985 to 1986, there was as yet no noticeable mix of races on the sands and that struck a sad note.

Natal's climate allowed us so much freedom to enjoy life outside. It was at such times as these weekends that it was easy to forget the havoc that could be wrought by extreme weather and other more earthly upheavals, but during the following year we were to be reminded that our marvellously stable climate and world could be subject to both. Before that, though, we would be experiencing a move of a more mundane but lasting kind.

MOVING FROM BYRNE TO RICHMOND

On the home front, things grew progressively worse. The house was not attracting buyers (it was that one bedroom issue coming back to bite us) and the bank was making noises about Bill's rising expense account. Unluckily for me, I was their first port of call and the fact that it was not my expense account didn't seem to cut much ice with them. The house was in both our names, so I suppose they thought I should share the blame.

As they saw it, Bill's overdraft couldn't meet the mortgage payments on its own and it needed my help. Not my kind of logic, but the ways of bankers are a mystery to me anyway. I would have loved to throw a tantrum and heap vitriol on she whom I believed to be the reason for Bill's mounting debt column, but I was far too English for that and proceeded to look for other solutions.

I decided to try and find a new job that would pay more and give me the means to even the balance a little. My plan meant I would need to go for interviews, which was something I couldn't keep quiet in a small town like Richmond. I thought I'd better warn the 'boys' of my intentions, or rather tell Peter and ask him to tell the others. This was always going to be hard as I loved my work there, mainly because of him and his avuncular good cheer. I broached the topic one morning after making him some coffee.

'Peter, I've got something I need to tell you.'

'Now, my girl, I wonder what that might be. Are you about to tell me you're going to be leaving us?'

'Oh dear, was it that easy to guess?'

'Well, I was only saying to John yesterday it's just a matter of time. With your hubby gone, it was clear you'd be looking for something better than this.'

'Nothing could be better than this, Peter,' I said with some feeling. 'It's just that you don't need me fulltime and now I need to work more hours. I can't afford not to anymore.'

'No worries, girl. We understand, although John will want to talk to you, I know.'

'Oh. Will he?'

'He's really the boss, you know. Don't worry. He's sorry, but like me, he's already realised you'll have to leave.'

I was nervous about talking to John as I'd never really found him easy. While he wasn't *un*kind at all, he wasn't what you would call kind*ly* and always maintained a distant reserve that was slightly forbidding. To make things worse, his desk was at the far end of the office, but it had a clear and commanding view of the front door. He was the only agent I could see when I entered the premises as all the others were in screened off cubicles down one side of the room. I was always aware of him watching even though he didn't say all that much – well not in my presence, anyway.

This being the case when I went to speak to him, I had to endure an uncomfortably long walk to his desk. As I approached, he leaned back in his chair, sucked on the

138

pipe that was never lit and regarded me under his rather hooded eyes. Hares in headlights had it easier. I was quaking by the time I reached his desk.

'So Val, you want to leave us, do you? Have you found another job already?'

I shuffled, feeling horribly awkward.

'No, not yet, John. I haven't even started looking, but I thought I should let you know. The thing is I need to work fulltime now.' He nodded. I took that as encouragement and soldiered on. 'And if I start going for interviews, you're going to know anyway. Richmond's bush telegraph will see to that,' I smiled in a feeble attempt at humour. To my relief, John chuckled.

'You're right there. Well, we'll be sorry to see you go, but yes, we understand.'

'Thank you. That's a big weight off my mind. I've been very happy here, and I don't actually want to go. But I have to and, well, I didn't want to leave you in the lurch.'

He nodded again.

'Would you just let me know as soon as you find something so I can look for a replacement for you? Jane can sit in for a while, but I know she won't want to do it long term.'

His face had gone back to distant and impassive again. If it hadn't been for the floppy farmer's hat, pipe and dusty shoes, he'd have made a powerful boardroom director, our John.

After mounting and struggling over this hurdle, I then faced the next one: finding that other job. Fortunately, I could now manage to type with four fingers on each hand. I still couldn't use my little fingers and typed with them stuck out like mini-ramrods but at least I could be honest when I was asked about my typing skills. I was reasonably accurate too, if not exactly a speed typist. My future employer could have one or the other, but not both.

I saw several jobs I would have liked in 'Maritzburg, but it was too far from the school. Although the appeal of a city salary had me dreaming of glorious independence, I couldn't even consider them seriously. My children needed me nearby and that was that. Then after a month or so of hunting, someone, I forget who, told me the local attorney, Mr Hugh Rethman, was advertising for a secretary who could copy type, act as receptionist and help with the debtors' payments and conveyancing.

I was very hesitant about applying at first. I had no experience with anything legal (apart from opening increasingly strident lawyers' letters about the house) and had to look up what conveyancing meant in the dictionary. Still it would mean a salary of R650 a month instead of the R375 I was currently earning, and it would be five days a week. Relatively, it would be a big increase in my income. I looked at the advert again. I can do that, I told myself. With Jodie at school every day, I would just have to find a solution for Mo. I breathed in, bit a few bullets and applied, half thinking and maybe even half hoping I wouldn't be asked for an interview. It would be a challenge; there was no doubt about that.

But Murphy was having some fun and decided that despite my misgivings, I should be put to the test. I received a call from a Miss Peggy Bernard, who sounded very posh and proper, asking if it would be convenient for me to call in the next afternoon to see Mr Rethman. I gulped, squeaked a 'yes' and agreed to an appointment before I could stop myself.

The attorney's offices were in a long single storey brick

building in Nelson Street, next to the Spar. Mr Rethman occupied one half of the building and the vet, Lyndsey Duncan, occupied the other. I knew her already as we'd been using her services to care for our animals. It seemed an odd combination, but not even I guessed at just how odd it would turn out to be. Symbiosis would gain a new meaning for me in the not very distant future.

The next day, I approached the office door at the allotted time and pushed it open. Seated at a desk facing me and just to the right of the entrance was a smiling face of very dark hue. The face stood up revealing the form of a man of small stature dressed in a black suit and snowy white shirt. I looked around; there was no one else in the room.

'Mr Rethman?' I asked, offering him my hand. In my nervous state, I just assumed he must be although if I'd stopped to screw my head on properly, I'd have known that in the South Africa of December 1985, that wouldn't have been possible.

He laughed, shaking his head while taking my hand in a rather soft clasp.

'No, madam, my name is Dlamini. I am Mr Rethman's legal assistant. Please to sit down,' he gestured to the chairs near him. 'I will inform Mr Rethman of your arrival. Would you care to imbibe some tea?'

I was already sitting by then. If I hadn't been, I'd have been bowled off my feet by his old world charm and quaint turn of phrase. He could have stepped out of a Dickens novel.

'No tea for me, thank you,' I replied, and then he disappeared through a door into what I supposed was the inner sanctum of Hugh Rethman's office.

A minute or so later, the door opened again, and a tall,

distinguished looking man with rather beautiful wavy grey hair came out. He wore a pale grey suit and a pink shirt and was more than slightly good-looking.

'You must be Valerie,' he greeted me. His smile seemed as cool and refined as the rest of him. I baulked. Another John, perhaps, but of the academic variety.

I got up, hoping my anxiety wouldn't betray me.

'Come in.' He waved a hand towards his office. I followed him in to a room that seemed incongruously untidy given his immaculate appearance. Every surface was covered in piles of files and books.

'Sit down,' he said, pulling an elegant visitor's chair out for me and lifting the heap of papers off it.

I sat. He sat. He looked at me with mild curiosity.

'So. Tell me. What can you do?'

Being shy by nature, it had taken me years to learn some social skills when meeting new people, but any kind of direct question still crippled me.

'Erm. What do you mean?' was all I could come up with. This was not going well.

'Well, I'm looking for a secretary and receptionist, so let's start with speaking, shall we? Would you be able to receive my clients? Professionally? Courteously?'

I felt everything going hot, even hotter than the temperature outside, which was already more than normal blood heat. I wanted to forget it all and wondered if he'd notice if I made a break for it. What saved me was a sudden spark of annoyance at the air of appraisal he assumed as he waited for my reply, although to be fair, I was probably over reacting. I was good at projecting my own insecurity on my interpretations.

'Yes, Mr Rethman. I *can* do that. I've been working at Richmond Estates for a year as *their* receptionist and secretary.'

'Oh? That's encouraging. So I take it you can type as well?'

'Yes, Mr Rethman.'

'What about the collections and conveyancing part?'

I hesitated. What were collections?

'Erm, I haven't done that before, but I'm sure I can learn.'

'Really? What qualifications do you have?'

'A Bachelor's degree.'

'In what?'

'English, history and French. For teaching.'

'Right,' he said. 'Suitably useless, but I suppose it shows you know how to think.'

My small bubble of self-confidence burst and evaporated. No one had ever before dismissed my years of study quite so succinctly. He was right, though. I couldn't blame him even if I wanted to. My qualifications had nothing to recommend them. I had zero relevant experience, so why on earth I ever thought I was fit for the purpose I had no idea. I felt all my 'can do' courage creep down into my shoes and hide.

The rest of the interview was a blur and when I left some minutes later, I was convinced I had failed. This was not going to be my next job. Twenty-four hours later, I had to change my mind. Peggy Bernard called me.

'Valerie? Is that you?' she asked after I'd answered the phone as usual with our phone number.

'Yes it is. Who's speaking please?'

'It's Attorney Rethman's offices, Peggy here. Mr Rethman asked me to call you to let you know the job is yours if you want it.'

'Oh? Really? Thank you! Erm, would you like my

answer now?'

She laughed.

'Well, yes, if that's convenient. If not, think it over and call me back tomorrow. But he'd like to know quite soon, in case he has to look for someone else.'

The rebellious half of me felt like telling her he could take his job and stick it somewhere unsavoury, but the other, rational and somewhat desperate half was pleased. So what if it was just because no one else had applied? At least he believed I had sufficient brains, if not skills. So I compromised.

'I'll just look over a few details and call you back in half an hour,' I answered, demurring only briefly. Actually, I was counting the minutes until I could grab the phone and dial the number.

And that's how I came to have a new job in Richmond. We agreed I should give the estate agency a month's notice and start in January. All I needed to do now that the Christmas holidays were upon us was to work out what to do about childcare.

As things transpired, the problem was swept from under me along with the house when the bank decided that my home was all theirs and not even half mine anymore. The details of what happened escape me now. I've no doubt buried them in a memory file marked 'do not open'. I have vague recollections of unpleasant meetings at the bank, even more unpleasant discussions with Bill, and signing lengthy legal documents, all of which culminated in my having to move out of the house and of Byrne with uncomfortable haste.

What I also don't remember is how I found out about

the house in Richmond that I managed to rent, but it all came together in a rush. While my luck was badly out on one hand, it was in on the other as the rented house was almost opposite the nursery school; it was fully furnished; and it came with a maid I was not allowed to dispense with. It also came with the not-so-added bonus of two small dogs.

The story behind my new home was a bit convoluted. I negotiated the rental through another attorney in Richmond. Mr Bev Nicholson was young, probably not much older than I was. He was also smiling, lively and friendly and made the whole process of leasing the house as smooth as my departure from the Byrne cottage was bumpy.

He was acting on behalf of an elderly lady who was going abroad for a year. She wanted to let the house out in her absence, the main reason being to have someone to look after her dogs and give her maid something to do. The rent was reduced as compensation for any inconvenience, which I thought was a gift from the gods at the time. The circumstances were all rather reminiscent of how I came to live on the farm just four and a half years earlier. But that was the only similarity. Life in Victoria Street, Richmond was completely different as I was soon to find out.

At the end of January, the girls, Microbe, Mitten and I were all installed. Brutus and Foggy went to live with Bill although Foggy didn't stay long. She moved out of his house and down the street to a luxury cluster home with a swanky Mercedes outside. That cat might have been born feral, but she knew which side her fish was fried. Apparently, Bill used to walk past the house and see her sitting in the window of her upmarket accommodation.

She would look at him as if she'd never seen him before.

I was sorry to be leaving Byrne. I would miss the Whites, Father Muller and Lindiwe although I knew I would hear news of them from Peggy, my new colleague. She also lived in Byrne but at the other end of the village, which explained why I'd never seen her. I was worried about Lindiwe's health but Peggy told me some of the other people Lindiwe worked for lived in her street, so she could find out how my former maid was faring with her TB. I would also miss Alex and my other neighbours, and even though the chances were that I'd bump into them at the school and in town, it wouldn't be the same.

Of course I could go and visit them in Byrne, but I knew that the further away we lived, the less likely we would be to venture out that way. As for going up to the farm, there would be even fewer opportunities to see Ouma and Oupa. Our lives were about to change substantially, especially as I was working full time. As it happened, I only saw them once or twice again before they moved away from Cottingham. 1986 was the end of an era in many ways. It marked the end of my rural life in Natal, and it also marked the end of the years of peace we had known in the area. Political trouble was about to escalate and with it came the start of violence.

It broke my heart to think of the bitterness that was spreading so fast among these vibrant, colourful people – people I'd grown deeply fond of. I remembered the mountain when we'd lived there; remembered Bongi calling across the valley to her sister at the *kraal*; saw Kheswa's grinning face when he told me I'd need to milk the cows for him, and Jabulani the gardener as he watered empty flower pots on what he thought were my instructions. I was frequently overwhelmed with regret

146

and sadness when I replayed conversations I'd had with Bongi as we ate together on the grass; how I'd teased her about her skin lightening efforts while we were so busy trying to get brown. Not only were our relationships with the people changing, but theirs with each other were too.

Hundreds of them lost their homes and jobs when the farmland was incorporated into Kwa-Zulu and they had to move to other townships outside 'Maritzburg and Richmond. And in Ndaleni, we heard of increasing conflict and faction fighting between the African National Congress (ANC) supporters and Inkatha, the supporters of Zululand's premier, Gatcha Buthelezi. The ANC was still a banned organisation at the time, but their followers mostly belonged to the United Democratic Front (UDF). Rumour had it that even Father Muller had been attacked. Things were beginning to turn ugly. The simple inter-dependence of the life we'd led among the Zulus on the farm and in the valley, and the interaction we'd shared with them, all that was becoming a thing of the past.

With so much going on, and with the people we loved leaving the area, I couldn't help thinking we were better off and safer in town.

LEARNING THE LAW BY MISTAKE

After we'd moved, life settled into some sort of rhythm. At home, there was Alice, my landlady's maid. She was large, and middle-aged, and I had the impression that she took a dim view of having a family of three foisted upon her when she was used to looking after one old lady. Raising a smile from her was pretty hard work, but to give her credit, she loved her employer – her real one, not me – and the two dogs, Timmy the Dachshund and Patches the Fox Terrier, so she did as she'd been asked and made sure they were fed and looked after.

For my part, I found them both chronically spoilt and even worse, they were not properly house-trained, so the morning routine now included dealing with the unpleasant offerings that greeted me in the lounge when I got up. Microbe should have been pleased to have the company, but she merely tolerated them, except if they came anywhere near me. She liked to lie at my feet in the evenings and neither of the other two was permitted to come within stroking distance of me. She might have been deaf, but there was nothing wrong with the sounds she produced. The message was very clear.

Dogs apart, Alice and I muddled along well enough. Since the nursery school only opened at eight and I had to get Jodie to Richmond Primary and myself to work before eight thirty, Alice took Mo across the road for me every morning and collected her at lunchtime. I also came home for lunch after picking Jodie up and Alice dished up a cooked meal. Sitting at the dining room table and eating in the middle of the day was not my idea, but it was what she was used to doing and I didn't like to disturb her regimen any more than I needed to. So we ploughed our way through boiled potatoes, green vegetables and whatever was on her own menu that day. It was probably very healthy given that it was all fresh and there wasn't a packet or a tin in sight, but it wasn't *haute cuisine;* nor was it ever exactly a taste sensation.

Alice was a bit dour, but she was a good soul although I have to say she was not Lindiwe, whose gentle ways I missed more than I was prepared to admit. In Victoria Street, I always had the feeling that Alice was in charge and we did what she said. Simple. It was a comical arrangement when I think about it now. If I'm honest, I found her a little intimidating and I tended to feel like a not altogether welcome guest. Not so the girls. In time, they got Alice's measure and teased her wickedly, which I think she secretly liked but would have paid a ransom in mealies rather than admit.

As for my job, I worked at Attorney Rethman's offices for a year and it was possibly the most interesting, stimulating and educational job I've ever had. It was also the most nerve-wracking.

Everything had to be ultra correct and error free and that wasn't only my typing. Allies were necessary and I found them in Dlamini and Peggy. They saved my bacon many a time in the first months. Peggy taught me everything I needed to know about conveyancing, which involved preparing the documents for property transfers. She was a demon proofreader, picking out every typo and errant comma like a sharp-eyed but kindly hawk, and I've benefited from her meticulous attention to detail ever since.

There was another employee in the office too. Eunice Hattingh was Mr Rethman's bookkeeper. She sat across from Peggy at the back of the office. The two of them were office pals and smoking partners and together they used to work, chatter and puff away in comfortable companionship. Eunice was only there a couple of days a week, but she was another character of great no-nonsense competence and her bookkeeping skills were without equal.

As for Dlamini, he gathered up the shreds of my confidence every time it collapsed – as it did quite often when it came to the collections, the other of my challenging tasks. In practice, it should have been simple. My job was to receive and record the money paid by debtors, many of whom came to the office to pay. It was fine when they gave me the correct amount, but quite often they didn't and I'd have to recalculate what they owed, plus costs, plus interest, plus goodness knows what else. It was the bane of my working day. I have always been useless with figures and even my parents were surprised when I passed my maths 'O' Level at school. I felt such a fraud for bluffing my way into the job when I knew I didn't have a clue. Dlamini, however, made sure I didn't make too much of a fool of myself. With his quaint speech, he was the archetypal Victorian gentleman and had the manners and graces to go with it.

'Dlamini, please, please can you help me with these collection calculations?' I begged him one day.

'Madam, I will endeavour to ameliorate your burden,' he replied. I just gaped at his response while he calmly set about sorting out the mess in the costs I'd been trying to add up. His language skills continued to fascinate me. On another occasion, I couldn't contain my curiosity as to where he'd acquired them.

I'd just burst into the office full of excitement.

'Do you know what I've just seen, Dlamini?'

'I would not presume to conjecture, madam.'

I hesitated, thrown off balance by his reply.

'Well,' I went on, resisting the distraction. 'I've just seen a goat going in next door!'

'Ah, but madam, it is the veterinarian's surgery. Perhaps it might not be considered so extraordinary to see a quadruped entering the premises.'

I looked at him in awe.

'Dlamini,' I said. I'm sure he had a first name, but I don't think anyone ever used it. 'You are unbelievable. Where did you learn to speak like that? Your vocabulary is astonishing.'

'Madam, you do me too much honour. I am a great admirer of classical language,' he said, waving a well-thumbed bible at me, his face grave. 'I have attempted to emulate its richness and range of expression.'

'Well, you do it with admirable success,' I told him, with equal gravity. Far be it from me to tell him context was everything. As for the vet's visitor, he was right. There was no reason why it was strange for a goat to be going in next door. I just wasn't expecting it and it looked so incongruous.

As far as Mr Rethman was concerned, he continued to be

Mr Cool in my eyes. My first impression didn't change much, although I came to realise he was a kind man even if he didn't show it too obviously. Looking back, he was more than likely just being professional. My previous work experience was limited to the estate agency and prior to that, sorting artefacts and documents in the archives of an English museum. Before that, I'd had a job restoring furniture. I knew little to nothing about real office life.

Nevertheless, having been plagued since childhood by inhibitions that I struggled to shake off, I continued to feel awkward and gauche in his presence. All I knew about his personal life were two things: that he was a keen sportsman and that he was married. It seems strange now, but I never had the nerve to ask about his family or his life. Peggy told me he was training for the Comrades Marathon and I'd see him on the road to Byrne at the weekends, pounding along for all he was worth. Running, it seemed, was an addictive pursuit, even for lofty legal types.

I admired him, all the same. I could see he was a good and deeply caring lawyer. As I remember it, many of his clients were Africans and as far as I knew, he only charged those that were poor if he won a case for them and when their costs were covered by an award from the court. He spent a large proportion of his time acting for them, and I believe he was pretty successful although he rarely spoke about it, not to me anyway.

Of course, I don't know any of this for sure, but it increases my respect for him in hindsight (always a great eye opener). Richmond became a dangerous place in the decade that followed and I can imagine my boss was fully aware of the risks involved in both defending and prosecuting different factions in the community. The only way I could ascertain how a case was progressing was by the faint smile on his face when he came back to the office if things had gone well and a frown if they hadn't. On these occasions, he would just disappear into his office. At better times, he would join us with his cup of tea and tell us amusing stories about some of his clients with great good humour.

Naturally, there were white clients too, but their issues were only occasionally criminal court matters and mostly involved things like civil claims for debts, property transfers, the drawing up of wills and administering trust accounts. It was a one-size-fits all law firm and I had so much to learn it was almost mind-boggling.

Mr Rethman was often at court, which gave me time to catch up, especially on the days Peggy wasn't there. On those days, and if Dlamini wasn't out on one of his own legal missions, I could ask him if I wasn't sure about something. He not only helped me with the collections process but also when I got stuck with details of the court documents I had to type out. Dlamini's main function was to interpret Hugh Rethman's legal council for his African clients so he held a highly responsible position. Many of the clients couldn't speak English and even though my boss spoke what sounded to me like pretty competent Zulu, he preferred to have Dlamini there as interpreter.

As soon as I arrived at work, I went into Mr Rethman's office to receive my daily instructions and take dictation. He liked to compose his letters verbally, and luckily for me, he spoke slowly and clearly so I could just write down what he said. I suppose he could have used a tape recorder, but he never did and thankfully, he never expected me to do shorthand. I'd have had to fake it if he had.

Anyhow, if there were any alterations, they were usually because he'd changed his mind and not because I couldn't keep up. So far so good. Then he would give me details of the various court documents I needed to prepare. These would range from summonses (mostly for debt) to warrants of arrest documents. In between, there would be default notices when the debtors didn't pay, warrants of execution as a prelude to sending the Sheriff of the Court (the Bailiff) round, and contempt of court notices when the defendant failed to meet the demands laid down by the court.

The final stage, the warrant of arrest, was the one I disliked doing as it could only mean one thing: the debtor hadn't been able to pay even the small instalment required by the court. Once the legal process started, that small amount would grow exponentially with every new notice and the poor soul would be increasingly unable to extract him or herself from what became a crippling debt. Often this meant the legal notices were ignored, and then the inevitable would happen. A warrant of arrest would be issued which resulted in imprisonment, and that was no help at all.

Most of the debtors were people who'd got into financial trouble just as most of us do – by spending more than we earn, or through bad luck. I knew the feeling very well and sympathised with them. I was after all dealing with the fallout from Bill's over optimistic attitude to money. It could happen to anyone, however well meaning. I counted myself lucky that I had a job that kept me out of the downward spiral and the endless legal processes that just added to the costs and made hauling oneself out of debt impossible.

I soon got into my stride with these documents, and I actually enjoyed typing them up as they looked professional and neat. I was even proud of my skills in laying them out correctly. I just didn't like what they represented. Funnily enough, I can still hear the sound of Mr Rethman's voice as he intoned the instructions.

'Right, Val, we have a Warrant of Execution next.' he'd start. 'So, normal heading please... in the Magistrate's court etc, case number 564/310. Then, in the matter of Ali Naidoo, plaintiff, vs Denis Visser, defendant (or whoever). Then, document title – warrant of execution against property.'

The name of the notice had to be set between two black lines more or less in the middle of the page to make it stand out. After this, and in typical legal language full of old-fashioned words like 'whereas', 'heretofore' and 'abovementioned', the details of the claim, the judgement and the amount to be raised against the defendant's goods were itemised.

All of this was for the Sheriff of the Court, or bailiff, whose job was to go to the defendant and formally attach goods to the value of the outstanding debt, meaning he would record a list of the property to be removed. Generally, this would be household items like furniture and appliances. It seemed to me that these were always the things guaranteed to make the debtor's life as miserable as possible. In fact, it didn't take me long to decide it was better not to think about the implications of what I was typing too much as I couldn't help being aware of how close I'd come to the same fate.

After I'd been there a few months, Mr Rethman bought a new typewriter. It was an amazingly modern electronic machine with a small very narrow display screen that extended from one side to the other just above the keyboard. I could see what I was typing on it just like the later full screen monitors; the only difference was that I saw just one line at a time. It was the last word in design and the newest technology on the market. The beauty of it was that it had spell check and delete functions and these were a dream. It took some getting used to at first, but I was thrilled with it. Not only did it make typing all the documents much faster, it saved reams of paper as I no longer had to start again when I made a mistake. And in spite of my improved skills, I still made scores of them. I can even imagine now that this was why Mr Rethman bought it in the first place; it must have saved him a fortune in waste paper.

Making mistakes was the major burden of my life in my early days there. At night I dreamt of panic scenarios where a contract had to be typed and sent off by some impossible and weird time limit my dream world cooked up. I made typos on every line, had to re-type pages time and again, sweating with anxiety, and all the while the nightmare clock was ticking away towards crisis time. Then I wouldn't be able to get it to the post on time because I'd forget to stamp it or lose my way or not be able to find my car. That type of dream.

The reality wasn't much better. I was learning the law by mistakes, my mistakes. Every day was like my nightmares; only I was well and truly awake. I think I must have used half a tree's worth of paper before I finally managed to type something error free the first time. The absolute worst tests were the conveyancing documents, especially the Deeds of Transfer. Luckily, it was Peggy who gave me these to do and she was a patient teacher. But I have to say that typing them up was worse than doing my final university exams, and I had to do at least one a week.

Peggy, I should mention, was also a remarkable soul. When I started at Mr Rethman's offices, she was already seventy-one. She was stout, but upright and as bright as a robin – as well as being hawk-eyed. She claimed to smoke twenty cigarettes a day and she said she drank two tots of whiskey every night. Far from having any health problems, she was as fit as a fiddle. She worked three days a week, and when I asked her if she ever felt like retiring, she scoffed.

'Why? Why does anyone think that not working is any more fun than working? I don't *want* to retire,' she said. 'I thoroughly enjoy my job, I like my boss and all of this keeps my brain busy. What on earth would I do at home all week?'

'I don't know, Peggy. But you have a garden and dogs and presumably you have hobbies too?'

'No, I don't. My dogs are my hobby. I take them for an hour's walk before work and again after work. Every day.'

'Well that explains why you're still so fit.' I looked at her puffing away on her cigarette, my surprise a bit too obvious.

She chuckled and nodded.

'You're right, you don't think I deserve it and it's true. I probably shouldn't smoke so much, but I'm sure the walking keeps me strong. And the whiskey of course.'

'The whiskey?'

'Yes, my dear. I drink my two tots entirely for

medicinal purposes, you know. I wouldn't do it otherwise.'

'Right,' I smiled at her, only just managing to resist a wink.

She just laughed, and puffed some more.

Apart from the nail-biting stress of my new responsibilities, the only real downside to working at Mr Rethman's was the heat. The building was modern and low ceilinged. It was also without any shade. Or any air conditioning. It was almost unbearably hot in the summer months and my desk was right next to the window. The only relief was that it was next to the door as well, which was open in very hot weather, something I doubt people would risk these days.

Even so, I would walk home at lunchtime feeling limp and soggy, then shower and put on fresh clothes before going back in the afternoon. By the end of the day, my clothes were sticking to me once again and I'd change as soon as I got home. In winter, the office was much more pleasant as the sun warmed us up nicely, but it was more often too hot than not.

There was one aspect of working at Attorney Rethman's that I loved although it had nothing to do with the law, or the weather, and everything to do with the animals next door. This was where the odd symbiosis of the two practices came in. The vet, Lyndsey, was a lovely bright girl who breezed in and out of our office through the side door without any reservation or compunction about breaching the lawyer's hallowed portals. It was easily done and we could have done the same to her if it weren't for the risk of contaminating her surgery while she was in mid operation.

The way the building was designed allowed for just

two toilets in one small room between the two premises. What this meant was that we shared the loos with Lyndsey and since we both needed access, we had connecting doors that were left unlocked while we were all at work. Lyndsey worked alone, so when she had quiet times she would pop in for a chat. Likewise, when she was very busy, she sometimes came to ask for help. On one occasion, Mo was with me at the office because she had a cold and couldn't go to play school. She was bored, she loved animals and she knew that Lyndsey was next door. The plea was inevitable.

'Mummy, can I go and see the vet?'

'No, sweetie. She's busy.'

'Please? It's boring here.'

'Mo, I said no, and that's that. Now I'm busy, so... '

But I never got to finish my sentence as at that moment, the gods answered Mo's prayers (as they usually did) and Lyndsey put her head round the door.

'Could someone come and help me hold this dog's legs out. I can't seem to keep them still and I need to stitch him up.'

'Can I go, can I go?' begged Mo, already half way to the door.

'Can she?' I asked Lyndsey.

'Yes, of course. She's welcome. That'll be great!'

So Mo disappeared to become a vet's assistant for half an hour. She wasn't even five years old but she still remembers the occasion. It wasn't the only time we were called on either. Mostly it was Peggy who went through as she was closest to the door, and she could make her own rules about devotion to duty, but I got to go now and then too and it made a welcome change in the day. As for Hugh Rethman, he never seemed to mind, which further proved he had his softer side.

Another occasional surprise was finding the loo occupied when we went in to do our business – but not by another person. The first time it happened, I went to open the door to the toilets as usual. My curiosity was piqued when I couldn't push it more than a few inches. There was something stopping it and it was right on the other side. I pushed a bit more and squeezed through the gap expecting to find a sack or bag of something, but instead, my obstruction struggled to its feet and said 'baaa' to me in a plaintive voice. There it was, a lamb in the loo. The poor little thing had a bandaged leg and shouldn't have been made to stand up at all.

I backed out and stuck my head round Lyndsey's door.

'Ahem, Lyndsey, is your guest going to be in the loo for long? The thing is, anytime someone wants to go, the poor baby will have to get up, and I'm sure that's not going to be good for him. Or is it her?'

'Oh I'm so sorry, Val. I didn't mean to leave her there, but I had to see a dog in a hurry and I don't have a cage big enough to put a lamb in. I'll come and get her now.'

'Ah, right. That's quite understandable. Yes. The loo makes a perfect sheep shed,' I laughed.

Lyndsey grinned, unrepentant despite her apologies, and followed me through to collect her patient.

Later on, I had my own reason to be glad of our relationship with Lyndsey. She came to my rescue and gave me the most amazing support when through a tragic accident I lost my beloved Microbe. One of my landlady's two dogs, Patches, was an escape artist supreme and had learnt how to open the windows in the lounge and jump out. There was no front fence to the bungalow, so having made his escape, he would run out into the road and chase cars and bicycles. He became a real menace, and I was at a loss as to how to keep him in. It was more than just embarrassing and more than once I found myself apologising to neighbours and passers-by for the little brat's aggression.

What made matters worse was that Microbe started to follow him. Being deaf, though, it was much more dangerous for her and this just added to my worries. I received reports from people saying they'd seen my dog wandering round the village, but she was always home when I got there – apart from the time she turned up at the office to find me. To my relief my boss found this amusing, but it couldn't go on. It was too risky. In desperation I set up a kind of low washing line in the garden and attached her lead to it. She could run up and down, but not get beyond the gate. That was the theory anyway.

In practice, it didn't help because the day came when Alice called me at work to tell me Microbe had been run over. Apparently Patches had broken out of the house again and roared out of the garden after someone on a motorbike. Microbe roared after Patches, broke her washing line and hurtled into the road straight under the wheels of a car. Being deaf, she hadn't heard it and therefore hadn't seen it. I crumpled. Microbe was my devoted little friend. She slept at my feet, lay next to my bed every night and followed me everywhere when I was at home. This was just too much. Without stopping to think, I headed for the passage between the offices and rushed into Lyndsey's rooms.

'Lyndsey, please, please can you help me?' I cried.

'Microbe's been run over and I don't have a car to get home.'

Before I'd even finished, Lyndsey had grabbed her keys and was starting for the door.

'Come on, we're going. Now.'

She drove me home where we found Microbe lying broken and bloody by the side of the road in front of the house. I still don't know how I held it together to help Lyndsey ease her on to a kind of stretcher and lift her into the back of her van, but we got her in and headed back to the surgery. Half an hour later, I knew there was going to be no more help for my faithful friend.

'She's too badly injured, Val. I've had to sedate her heavily or she'd be in unbearable pain, but she's got internal injuries and bleeding. I'm so sorry. There really isn't anything I can do that would be any guarantee of success. And it would take weeks and weeks of operations and treatment.'

I knew what she was saying. I couldn't afford all the treatment she'd need. She knew it. I knew it. There really was only one possible decision.

Gulping down the tears, I held Microbe in my arms while Lyndsey put her gently to sleep. I couldn't believe she'd gone; it was like losing Cindy all over again. But for Microbe, it was the kindest thing to do under the circumstances. After it was over, Lyndsey showed once again what a wonderful friend she was. Knowing I didn't have the resources, she dealt with Microbe's burial. I don't even know how she did it, but I do know that somewhere in the garden of the house in Victoria Street lie the remains of my little Dalmation. She was a lovely, loyal, strong-hearted dog, but her deafness was eventually her undoing.

The rest of my year as a legal secretary passed without any further incidents that I can recall. I imagine I got used to the routines and eventually the work must have become much easier through constant practice. My anxiety diminished and I suppose even my calculation skills must have gradually improved as well. I know I found it endlessly interesting and was daily grateful that Hugh Rethman had taken a chance on this quite well educated but sadly unskilled employee. I am thankful for what he, Peggy and Dlamini taught me to this day and of all the jobs I've had in my life, it has been the most useful; the language of the law I learned there still serves me well in my business English teaching today. That aside, there were various other things going on in life and the world that marked the year out as significant – for me, anyway. Some of these were of a natural and quite phenomenal kind.

UPHEAVALS BOTH EARTHLY AND OTHERWISE

The climate in South Africa is largely stable, but largely is the key word here. Each region of the country has differences in climate and only the Western Cape can be said to be truly variable, although that doesn't mean the other regions don't have their periods of instability and extreme incidents. In general, Kwa-Zulu Natal has what many people consider to be a year-round holiday climate and Durban, its largest city, boasts over 300 days of sunshine every year. But even in such an ideal climate, weather with a capital W can occur.

In the time I spent in Byrne and Richmond, we had our usual share of torrential downpours, sudden wind squalls and hail. These were just normal fare when judged against the freak Christmas frost we'd experienced in Byrne. They were also just the subject of local discussion when we would compare notes on where we were and what we were doing when the relevant cloudburst occurred. As for other types of extreme weather, I heard about, but never experienced, the occasional tornado in our area although one of these came a little too close for comfort. It tore through a village not too far from the Byrne valley as the crow flies and destroyed everything in its path. It even sucked the engine out of a truck and hurled it hundreds of metres, like a giant tossing out a piece of rubbish. I was thankful I'd never been in the path of one of these spiralling furies, but they weren't and aren't uncommon in South Africa. Some of them didn't even make the news other than regionally

In January 1984, however, I witnessed first hand the effects of the devastating cyclone Domoina and later in February, its smaller cousin, Imboa. The torrential rain the former brought with it resulted in the flooding of huge areas of northern Natal, Swaziland and Mozambique. It also swelled rivers further south to bursting point, washing away bridges and depositing deep layers of sediment on adjacent land causing extensive crop damage in the process. Bill was actually in Swaziland when Domoina struck and couldn't get home without heading west towards Johannesburg and doing a huge round trip.

Later on, I saw for myself the damage these torrents and deluges caused; they left me aghast at the devastation. We'd been up to Richard's Bay on the north coast and standing on a river bank in the north of the province, I looked at all that was left of the bridge that used to span it. There was just a jagged edge like a broken off outcrop, and the white centre line of the road pointed incongruously into the yawning space beyond. The bridge itself could just be seen lying in the river bed a few hundred metres away.

'This is scary,' I said to Bill. 'Just imagine if you didn't know the road wasn't here!'

There was just a sign at the side of the road about fifty metres from the edge; otherwise, there was nothing to warn the unwary driver and no barrier against hurtling into the abyss.

When Imboa arrived about a month later, more heavy

rains washed away temporary bridges built after Domoina and caused further misery to the thousands of people already made homeless or stranded by the earlier storm.

During the year I spent in Richmond, nothing so destructive as these cyclones occurred, but that didn't mean the storms we suffered were not frightening or potentially life-endangering. The standard summer downpours alone could bring with them thunder and lightning that in my previous life in England would have had me hiding under the stairs. Fork lightning was commonplace in South Africa and I was told that more South Africans died from lightning strikes than from snakebites or any other natural hazard. This was serious business and made our European thunderstorms seem rather paltry.

On one occasion before Bill moved away, he was driving along the dirt road towards Elandskop when he heard a loud crack and saw searing blue flashes on either side of his car. Shaken but unharmed, he realised he'd just driven between two forks of lightning that hit the road simultaneously on either side of him. He was very unnerved by the experience and the electrical charge he'd felt made him feel unsettled. It was days before he talked it out of his system, by which time the story had developed somewhat and the forks had become a fiery tunnel he'd seen arching over the road before he drove through it. The imagination is a wondrous gift, isn't it?

Some time later, while the girls and I were in Richmond, I agreed to drive them up to Johannesburg for the half term holiday to stay with Bill and his girlfriend. We drove up in the little half-loaf bus. All went well until we reached the approaches to Johannesburg. My 'mom's taxi' chose this moment to start coughing and spluttering and it was in a state of some anxiety that I eventually arrived where Bill lived in the city's suburbs with a somewhat sick vehicle and two tired and fretful children. As I had to get back again and didn't want to risk using the van, Bill lent me a *bakkie* for the drive home, agreeing to have the half-loaf checked out. I was vexed about the situation, I know, but I came to be grateful that my little bus had let me down on this occasion. It was providential; I don't think I'd have made it back in one piece had I been driving it.

In those days of no Internet, we were not nearly so in touch with the news, so what I didn't know was that a furious storm was blowing up in Natal and somewhere around Ladysmith on the N3 in the Natal Midlands, I drove into it. Suddenly the world turned dark and I entered some kind of awful maelstrom. It was both terrible and terrifying. The wind buffeted and rocked the *bakkie* on the road and the rain poured down in torrents. It was so bad I could barely see a few metres in front of me. I had to peer through the windscreen as branches and debris flew past and the rain bounced violently off the bonnet.

Until quite recently, I believed this too was a tropical storm at the very least, but I can find no record of anything worthy of mention in old news or weather accounts. So be it. I can only begin to imagine how bad a real cyclone must be if what I experienced that night was nothing of note. Fortunately, the *bakkie* sat low on the road and was much less susceptible to side winds than my light, high-sided Suzuki half-loaf. I dread to think what would have happened if I'd been driving it; the first big gust would have had it over. As it was, I crawled through to 'Maritzburg and was almost pathetically relieved when I turned onto the Richmond road.

Even then, I had to drive at a painfully slow speed and with extreme care. In my headlights, I saw trees bent sideways in the wind and branches lay scattered across the road, tossed around by the gusts. Despite having much less traffic than the highway, it was dangerous going, what with the obstacle course, the pounding rain and my fear of having to swerve round a fallen tree or branch when something was coming the other way. I imagined all kinds of Hammer horror film fantasies and was a wreck by the time I arrived back in Richmond.

But as these things go in South Africa, the next morning the sun was shining and all was calm again. Except for the mess of evidence lying in the roads, fields and gardens, I could have believed I'd dreamt it all. Although my storm might not have made the news or the long-term records of serious and damaging weather occurrences, it was the worst I'd ever experienced and I've never forgotten it.

But that was weather, one kind of phenomenon. Another natural event that was to be a first for me in 1986 was an earthquake. The records have it that it happened on October the 5th and that its epicentre was in the Transkei, close to the town of Kokstad and geographically just down the road from Richmond. This is something I've only confirmed through research quite recently because if anyone had asked me even a year ago, I would have told them the quake took place off the Natal coast. I don't know why I thought so; it's just what's been rooted in my mind all these years. But its location isn't really important from my perspective. Those of us who were affected knew that it had definitely occurred and that it caused some fairly significant damage in the Richmond area.

The other reason I was so sure of it was because I felt it happen. It was quite late in the evening, somewhere between eight and nine. Being a Sunday night, the girls were both in bed and I was heading that way myself. We nearly always went to bed quite early in Richmond anyway, mainly because we were also up early in the morning. It was a different rhythm of life from the one I was used to in Europe.

I'd tidied up, bathed and was just letting the dogs out for a final run round the garden when suddenly my world started to roll like a boat on the waves. I thought I was having a fainting fit at the very least and held on to the doorpost to stop myself falling. But then the dogs shot inside and cowered under the table and I realised it wasn't me.

The sensation of rolling on waves continued for a few seconds more but before my alarm grew to panic proportions, it stopped. Everything went back to normal and barring a few skew pictures on the walls, it was as if nothing had occurred at all. Shaken, I checked on the girls. They'd slept through it, thank heavens. Then I checked the walls, doors and windows. To my surprise, and relief, nothing was broken or even cracked. I started to think I'd imagined things but the crooked pictures and the shivering mutts convinced me I hadn't. After straightening everything, soothing the poor dogs and fiddling around for a while, as one does in times of stress, I decided there wasn't going to be a repeat. It must have been a one-off, whatever it was. It still hadn't registered

I'd experienced an earth tremor and as I didn't hear any activity outside, I locked up and went to bed.

The next morning, I mentioned it to Alice when she arrived. She'd come in from Ndaleni on one of the combi-taxis; the mini buses that were widely used as public transport. She told me everyone in the township was talking about the grumbling earth.

'It is a sign, madam,' she said. No Bongi-style 'Missy Val' for me from Alice either. She, like Lindiwe, was much too formal.

'A sign? But of what? I mean was it really an earthquake?'

'Yes, madam. Many houses in Ndaleni broken.'

'Broken? Oh no! Is it bad?'

'Not very bad, but not good also.' I realised her English didn't run to synonyms and assumed she meant to say they'd suffered some minor damage. But then she added a warning.

'Bad things are coming here, madam. We feel this.'

It wasn't so surprising that she and others might think along these lines. There was growing tension in the townships between the youth looking for faster change and the old Zulu guard. There was also the possibility that some tribal issues were being labelled with political banners, and this was a potent combination. I knew little about what was really going on in the townships; none of us did, although I was aware that the peace that had formerly reigned in the area was crumbling rapidly and divisions were growing in the community. These tensions were only increasing with the growth of the informal townships too. Dispossessed farm workers, such as those who used to live on the Ellenses' farm were being forced into township life and this couldn't be helping matters.

An earthquake at this time might well be seen as a prophetic sign of trouble to come.

When I got to school with Jodie there was also talk of the quake, but it was much less loaded and more focused on the damage done.

'I heard quite a few houses got some cracks in their walls,' one of the mothers told me. 'We didn't have any damage ourselves, but I have to say it was just the weirdest feeling. Did you have any problems,' she asked me.

'No, nothing, but you're right about weird.' I agreed. 'It felt as if the house was on a boat, the way it was rolling!' We chatted some more and I told her about Alice's feelings of premonition; that it was a bad omen.

'*Ja*, well, she could be right there. Things are not going well between the UDF and Inkatha and there's also growing resentment against us as well. I don't know how long we'll be staying here to be honest.'

I didn't like to show too much ignorance, so I nodded and just listened to what she was saying with some unease. And then I remembered an encounter I'd had just a few days before. It was nothing, but it was everything too.

I was walking along Victoria Street, heading towards the centre and a man was coming towards me. Whether he was a local Zulu or from elsewhere, I wouldn't know, but as he passed me, he gave me a look of such intense hostility it shook me. It was the first time I'd ever been greeted with any animosity by anyone in the area. It was new to me and it made a deep impression; so much so that the image of his face has remained with me all these years. If Alice was taking the earthquake as some kind of manifestation of other energies in conflict, perhaps we should be doing so too. It was certainly food for thought and it was something that occupied my mind quite frequently in the months to come. Upheavals could come in many different forms.

THE END OF THE ROAD

By January 1987, I had made the decision to leave Richmond. I don't know if the fates were taking a hand in my departure but it proved to be timely although my reasons for closing the chapter on my life in Natal had little to do with the increasing unrest. That isn't to say it didn't trouble me. The creeping awareness that the peaceful world in which we'd lived for so many years was disintegrating disturbed me as well as many others, I know. There was a sense that we were all losing something precious; that our tranquil life was irrevocably slipping away. It was as if the two political giants, Inkatha and the ANC/UDF, were slowly awakening. And they were not only snarling at each other but lashing out too.

What's more, they were directing their ire at all of us. All the same, up to the time I left there were no major incidents in Richmond that I can recall, not outside the townships in any event. Most of the uprisings during 1986 took place closer to 'Maritzburg in the Edendale area following a national State of Emergency that was declared in June. The worst conflicts in Richmond only came later after I was well out of the way.

But to return to the end of my particular road, my realisation that it was time to draw a line through my

Natal years, to pack up and leave, was prompted much more by personal circumstances. Being so, they do not belong to these recollections and it is enough to say that I was finding single motherhood much more difficult than I'd anticipated, especially without a support system.

Bill and I had come to South Africa as adults and we had no family nearby. Of those that were in the country, they were distant relatives of Bill's and we'd never met them. While we lived on the farm, I'd felt that the Ellenses were our family; they were certainly as caring as any parents and I loved them as dearly. But in moving to Byrne, we'd struck out on our own and left their kind and supportive guidance. And then by 1987, they'd moved to Howick anyway where they were closer to facilities, neighbours, doctors and help if needed; by that time, they were quite elderly, both being in their early eighties.

My dilemma was that I was working full days and didn't have the energy or time to give my daughters the attention they needed; in a nutshell, they were running more than a little wild. What made things worse was that poor Alice was the victim of their misdeeds. She was not used to looking after wilful children and the more she tried to control them, the more they enjoyed evading her.

One example of their mischief involved a spot of breaking and entering that caused me intense embarrassment as well as worry. In hindsight, it was just a symptom of their high spirits. I didn't see it that way then, particularly when faced with Alice's rather formidable anger, which had both her bulk and volume behind it.

The house where we were living was a plain, single storey home with a large open-plan lounge-cum-dining room and three bedrooms. When my landlady left, she kept one of the bedrooms into which she locked all her personal and precious possessions. To us, it was the secret room and the girls were forbidden to enter it. In a sense I too was banned as officially Alice was the only one to have a key, even though she kept it in the kitchen where I could easily find it. The issue should have ended there, but it didn't.

It all happened one day when Alice left the window of the secret room open. It was something she would do from time to let the air in but as the summer months grew warmer, she opened it more often. Now this particular window was at the back of the house beyond which was a small patch of ground where Alice grew her own maize. Being such tall plants with thick stalks and lavish leaves, the 'mealie patch' was a wonderful and natural maze (excuse the pun) where my young things could play hide and seek; they also used it to escape from Alice.

I don't know which of the girls noticed the open window first; one of them must have seen it and got a bee in her bonnet because what happened next was that they climbed in and started larking about in the prohibited but exciting realms of our landlady's furnishings, bedding and knick-knacks.

When Alice discovered what they were up to, she was almost apoplectic with fury and chased them out with threats of summoning the *tokoloshe* – a dire punishment indeed, because the *tokoloshe* is an evil spirit from Bantu mythology whose main task seems to be to scare children. Since legend claims it has a habit of hiding under beds, many suspicious Africans will raise their beds on bricks to make sure these nasty creatures can't remain unseen. In spite of this menacing warning, my daughters hadn't shown any remorse and simply scurried out of her way, most likely giggling, which would have enraged her still further.

The result was that when I arrived home, my 'home executive' (she was much more in charge than any maid) was in a state of high dudgeon.

'Madam,' she said with great deliberation. 'Your children, they are very bad.'

I was taken aback by the vehemence.

'Oh, why, Alice? What have they done?'

'They go into other madam's room and make big mess. That is why. Very bad children. Very, very bad.' She jabbed a finger at me with every 'very'.

Squashing an almost irresistible urge to laugh, which was most likely nerves now I come to think of it, I had to agree. I was genuinely horrified. What if they'd damaged anything?

'Will you show me, Alice? If they've broken anything I mean?'

'Nothing broken, madam. No, I don't think it. But big, big mess,' she repeated, bustling into the kitchen to fetch the key. It was hanging on a hook high up on the inside of a cupboard door and being quite ample, she had trouble stretching up to reach it. She then led me down the passage to the room. Looking at that firmly closed door before she unlocked it, I realised how tempting it must have been. There'd been many times I wanted to take a peek into it too. After all, the forbidden is somehow much more attractive, isn't it? Despite my general exhaustion, I wasn't so old and jaded I couldn't see that too.

Alice was exaggerating, but only slightly. As I looked into the room, I could see clothes, ornaments and suitcases piled up on a bed, while other items of furniture, including chairs and lamps, were pushed into a corner. To me, it seemed a fairly disorganised collection anyway, but it was the tent the girls had made on the floor out of blankets and chairs that made it look chaotic. Inside the tent were cushions and books and other sundry items that were part of some fantasy world they'd invented.

'Oh dear, I am sorry, Alice. I'll speak to them, I promise, but first, let's tidy this up. You are right. They've been very naughty indeed, but it looks worse than it is.'

She grumbled on, complaining about how ill behaved my daughters were and how they hadn't been sorry at all, which was almost certainly true. I'm not sure if she accepted my apologies or soothing words, but together we folded up the blankets and put the various items back where we thought they'd come from. Alice locked the door with extra emphasis and returned the key to its hook. I then sought out my errant offspring to hear their side of the story.

'We couldn't help it, Mama,' Jodie explained. Calling me 'Mama' instead of 'Mum' was tactical. 'The window was wide open, and well... we just had to.' She looked at me with big earnest eyes. But her sister gave the game away. Mo started giggling.

'Alice was so cross, Mummy. She puffed up like this.' She blew out her cheeks and hunched her head into her shoulders, doing a fair impression of the Incredible Hulk, a monster they'd seen in a popular series that was frequently repeated on TV. Seeing her sister with eyes, face and neck bulging as if she were about to explode made Jodie start giggling too. Within seconds they were both helpless. Repentance was not going to happen, but after extracting their confessions, I made them eat humble pie with Alice. They did their best so although neither of them sounded at all sincere, I hoped that would be the end of it. Sadly it wasn't.

The next time, they stole the key off the hook in the kitchen cupboard. Again, I don't know which one noticed it was there, but between them they found a way to climb up and get it. The fun was then to unlock the 'secret room' and lock the door from the inside. With the window closed too, Alice couldn't reach them and was once again fuming. This time I was equally livid. I could no long ignore the fact these children of mine needed more supervision.

In retrospect, I can see they were just having a wonderful time with true childlike innocence. It was all about building playhouses and having tea parties; that was all there was to their wickedness. On the farm and in Byrne, they'd never had much in the way of games and toys and they'd learnt to make their own amusements using whatever was available. They continued to do so in Richmond, which only made the locked room even more appealing. It was tantalisingly *un*available.

I should also add that in the 1980s, there was very little TV during the day. We had a black and white set in the house, but programmes only started quite late in the afternoon. We hadn't owned one before, which made it an exciting novelty and like most children, mine loved it. I remember clearly the day I came home and found Jodie watching the pre-programme test screen, as if she could will the day's shows to start. Given these restrictions and the lack of other laid-on amusements, they were pretty resourceful. But in the case of the secret room, their creativity went just a little too far.

Another problem I had with the house was the

cockroaches. The kitchen was alive with them, and I could never figure out why. Alice cleaned up well and there was never any food left out, but as soon as darkness fell, out they would come in force. I came to dread going into the kitchen at night because the moment I turned on the light, dozens of the horrible creatures would scuttle back into the dark corners from which they'd crept. I just stood watching them in a kind of nauseous disgust. Luckily, they weren't very big, but the numbers were what repelled me. I tried everything to eradicate them, but nothing worked. It was all part of the pressure adding to my stress levels. I started being negative about the house. It was not mine and I missed having my own place, a feeling only intensified by my dislike of Patches, the little dog I couldn't help blaming for Microbe's death.

On top of this, I wanted to see my family. I hadn't been back to England since 1984 and my sister was due to give birth to twins at the end of January. I was also acutely aware that my father was getting old and living alone in sheltered housing in London. Add to that two brothers with children who were growing up without ever seeing their aunt and cousins in Africa and my list of concerns became compelling. I needed some time with them, to recharge my batteries and find out what I really wanted to do with my life. It would be good for my girls to go back to their roots and be with real family for a while. I wasn't divorced, but I was very much on my own. It was time to make a change.

What followed that decision happened in something of a rush and is consequently a little blurred. I gave in my notice to Hugh Rethman; I also told Mr Nicholson I was moving out of the house. As I recall, I had a year's contract, so it would have been coming to an end anyway. Everything told me it was time to move on.

One thing I remember much more clearly is saying my own farewells to the mountain where I'd been so happy for the first three years of my life in South Africa.

I drove out of Richmond, through Byrne and up the rocky, rutted dirt road until it rounded the last steep bend to the highest point. Just before it dropped down to Cottingham Farm, I braked and sat with car door open looking out onto the receding folds of the Natal Midlands' hills and on to the jagged peaks of the Drakensberg beyond. I drank it all in for the last time: the singing air, the spicy scent of the earth, and the mysterious grandeur of the panoramic scenery. Then I turned my eyes to Cottingham. The old house with its wide verandas lay in its dell, dreaming in the sunshine. It was empty of people and its solitary grace was deeply poignant. I couldn't bring myself to go there; to break the spell. I wanted to remember it from this distance, where I couldn't see if anything had already changed. That would happen anyway, for the next time I came to Natal, the house had long gone, demolished to build other homes in the growing townships; nothing but a few stones remained.

On another day, I said goodbye to Byrne village. It too had been a good place and despite the sad circumstances of our leaving, I was still fond of the little house in Charles Street. Getting out of the car, I stood and looked over the fence remembering it as I'd first seen it. There were new residents and it looked occupied, but so far nothing else had changed. The plum tree in the front garden was covered in fruit; the grass was trimmed and the whole house looked welcoming with its white paintwork and cottage pane windows. Over to the left, Father Muller's caravan still stood on his immaculate plot next door, so I had to assume he was still visiting and that the rumours he'd been attacked were just that. I hoped so anyway. It all looked the same and while I didn't feel the waves of nostalgia for Byrne that I did for the farm, I had pangs of regret that it had been such a short-lived dream.

Apart from the house, there were people in Byrne who were dear to the girls and me and we visited as many of them as possible to say we were leaving. In the years since, I've often wondered how the Whites fared and whether Father Muller lived to retire to his village caravan. And what of Alex and Bruce? Did they stay on in their orange groves when the world around them imploded? As for Lindiwe, I can only hope she survived, not just her TB but also the troubled times that followed.

Looking beyond Richmond, we took a trip to Durban for a last weekend with Helen and Tom. Always welcoming, always kind, they gave us a wonderful time and a memory to carry with us of a cheerful and optimistic gathering in the dappled sunlight of their beautiful garden. There were other friends to see in Durban too; friends who'd been part of my life with Bill. Because of these partings, our last two months in Richmond were spent on something of an emotional rollercoaster. I needed to go, but with so much heartfelt warmth, it was very tempting to stay.

As for my work, I knew I would miss it and all the colleagues I'd come to value so highly: Eunice Hattingh, the accounts magician; Peggy Bernard, my mentor who, despite her no nonsense brusqueness, was one of the kindest and fairest people I knew; Lyndsey the best of all vets, and dear Dlamini. I would have liked to give him a hug, but I know it would have crippled him with embarrassment. Then lastly there was my enigmatic boss, Hugh Rethman, to whom I was more grateful than he might ever have known. His principles set the standard of integrity I have used as a yardstick for much of my life since then. It says a great deal that I remember my work as a legal secretary so vividly and appreciate how much I have drawn on the skills I gained there over the years.

For the disposal of our household goods, I held what would today be called a garage sale. In South Africa, second-hand goods were currency and as long as the price was right, anything could be sold. I put all the things we couldn't take with us out on the drive with price stickers on them. Before long, throngs of local maids in their colourful overalls and bright scarves were sifting through our possessions, feeling, sizing and inspecting every item with loud commentary and often ribald laughter. Inevitably, the price stickers came off, so it was a question of some brisk bargaining on something like the following lines:

'How much for these plates, Mama?'

'Erm, two Rands fifty?'

'No, Mama, too much. I give you one Rand.'

'How about two Rands for the plates and these mugs too?'

'Okay, okay.' More laughter would seal the deal. 'Yes. Here, two Rands, and do you have paper, Mama? For wrapping?'

And so it went on. The trading was fast and furious and everything down to the last teaspoon and plastic doll was open to negotiation. What didn't sell was given away and what was left after that ended up in the rubbish.

Watching the women rummaging through the jumble of goods brought a lump to my throat. I would miss these people as well. They were so spontaneous and elemental in their noisy laughter and quick-witted banter. Their whole bodies shook with mirth. But I knew there was the other side too; the explosive anger that could sometimes be fatal. I would never forget the day when Bill came home white-faced with shock and told me one of his favourite employees was dead, stabbed by his brother-in-law during a row over a paltry debt of less than one Rand. This was the way of these country people. There was no inhibition in their responses to either joy or anger. I knew I would think of them with warm nostalgia in the months to come.

When it came to the final arrangements, my cat Mitten had already gone to Johannesburg to join Bill, along with the half-loaf van and the small collection of special things I wanted to keep. The girls had also gone to Johannesburg while I tidied up the loose ends in Richmond and said goodbye to the dogs and to Alice. She was probably relieved to see us go but put on a good act of looking sad. Standing in the doorway and waving to me as I backed out of the driveway, she gave me the traditional Zulu farewell of '*hamba gashle*', which is pronounced 'gashlé', and means 'go well' or 'go safely'. Who knows? Maybe she really was touched by the moment.

Finally, on March the 18th, 1987, my daughters and I arrived in London to a bone-chilling, grey and dismal day and for a day or two I wondered what on earth I had done. Had I really exchanged all that vibrancy, warmth and brightness for this washed-out, featureless world? It was a major culture and weather shock, but luckily I didn't have time to dwell on it for too long. We were quickly embroiled in the need to find somewhere to live, a school for the girls and a job for me. My father became my greatest support and having us there revitalised him tremendously. Even better, I was able to see my sister and one of my brothers on a regular basis. After we settled in, life settled down. For a while.

As things later turned out, this wasn't the end of my South African story. While I enjoyed my work as a medical insurance service assistant in London, and even though it did us all good to be with close family, I missed South Africa, and my daughters did too. It seemed the longer we stayed in England, the more we pined for the sunshine, the sunny people, the outdoor lifestyle and the sheer addictive magic of Africa. There was also a small matter of a marriage that wasn't resolved. So it was to nobody's great surprise that before the year was out, we were planning to go back again. This time, however, we didn't return to Natal; we started the second phase of our South African life on the *highveld* or the Reef, which is how the whole Johannesburg and Pretoria urban conglomeration was known.

To sum it up, I lived in Johannesburg permanently until the end of the nineties and then off and on until 2001. As for Natal, I didn't return to Richmond and Byrne again for many years. When I heard the news reports and looked on from the relative safety of Johannesburg, I was thankful I was so physically removed from the violence that marked the collapse of our idyll, but even then, I didn't know just how bad it was. That knowledge has

184

only come to me recently. Life in Johannesburg, the industrial and commercial heart of the country, was a different world altogether. It occupied our energies and our previous life in Kwa-Zulu Natal receded into the background. As a family, we experienced the big bad city with all it had going for and against it.

But that, as the saying goes, is another story altogether.

EPILOGUE

As a tribute to all those who lived on in Richmond after I left, and also to those who died, I feel it's time to say something about what happened in the period that followed my departure. Despite not living in South Africa any longer, I have never lost the affection I had for this area of Kwa-Zulu Natal and its people, and the story of the Richmond troubles should not be forgotten.

I don't want to end my South African recollections on a negative note as I still have great hopes that life in rural Kwa-Zulu Natal is slowly returning to normal, or at least that it will do so eventually. Even so, the fact that it went through more than a decade of upheaval that cost many people their lives can't be avoided. At the risk of being overly simplistic, I will just try to sum up what happened in the province in general and Richmond in particular. This isn't easy and I have to confess I still find it hard to follow; it really was incredibly complicated but I hope what I describe makes some kind of sense.

I will first acknowledge that the unrest we spoke about at the time, those 'rumblings' I referred to in the previous chapters, began quite early in the eighties in the townships around Pietermaritzburg. The fact that I didn't know much about it then other than rumour and hearsay is understandable given the limitations of our news and media access on the farm and in Byrne. After all, where we were it was very peaceful and our farming community was unaffected in those early years. We were also restricted by what the government of the day permitted journalists to report and broadcast, and as with all state subsidised organisations, the SABC had its own brand of 'news speak'.

These days it is much more difficult not to know what is happening; the Internet makes communications so much easier. At the time, we just heard talk about 'unrest in the townships'. I cannot speak for others but I accepted the salve that it was 'black on black' violence and therefore nothing to do with us. It sounds appallingly smug now. However, it was how things were in the context of the time and while living on the farm, I didn't look further than my own environment anyway; it was so removed from the harsh realities of the urban world. Nonetheless, I think it's maybe true to say that many of us were at worst blinkered and at best naïve. As for that word 'unrest'? It was so much more palatable than 'war'. But how did it all begin?

Under apartheid in South Africa, there were a number of so-called independent homelands. They were autonomous and had their own governments and presidents. The Transkei where we used to go on holiday in the early eighties was one of these. It had its own border controls and we needed to have our passports stamped when we crossed into it on the way to Port St John's. Kwa-Zulu in Natal was different; it was not independent. It consisted of large areas of the province, which were also known as Zululand, and while it had its own government and even a king, it was not separated from apartheid South Africa in the same way as the independent homelands.

In very basic terms, this seems to have been the crux of the problem in Natal. When I was living there, the Kwa-Zulu government was dominated by the Inkatha Freedom Party headed by Mangosuthu Buthelezi. Inkatha was characterised by its traditionalist approach and followed tribal organisation in many ways. If you like, they were the conservatives. On the other side of the Natal political coin, we had the United Democratic Front, an organisation that attracted politicised urban youth many of whom were followers of the banned ANC too. You could call them the socialists as their aim was for a united, non-racial and egalitarian society.

Many of the UDF/ANC supporters saw the Kwa-Zulu government, and for that read Inkatha or IFP, as an ally of the apartheid regime. Tensions had already been rising between them before the nation-wide State of Emergency was declared in 1986, the reasons for which are too complex to explain here. After this, though, it was down hill all the way and despite the State of Emergency measures, violent clashes between the two escalated in the townships around Durban and Pietermaritzburg where most of the black and Indian people lived. Before long the Edendale area west of Pietermaritzburg was also split by these conflicts.

Inevitably, it spread to the more rural areas and from 1989 to 1994 there was some bitter fighting between followers of the two parties in and around Richmond. Far too many people lost their homes, their livelihood and even their lives and it wasn't confined to the townships either. Farms were being attacked in growing numbers; many farmers and their employees were killed. In 1994 the elections settled the matter to some extent when the

ANC won control of Richmond and the conflict subsided. Sadly, however, those leading the ANC itself became divided and once again violence erupted in 1997 when a popular local and regional ANC leader was expelled from the party on charges of being a police spy. A mini-civil war ensued. The resulting spree of murders and fighting reached terrible and tragic levels.

There are many theories behind what fuelled the tragedy. Some blame personal power struggles, others focus on a 'third force' of white agent-provocateurs intent on perpetuating the disruption, and others put it down to long held tribal conflicts disguised by political banners. Had Kwa-Zulu been an independent homeland, it might never have escalated to the extent it did, but I don't know. I am no expert, nor have I steeped myself in the history of the region. All I can say is that those who stayed were very brave to do so and I can only be thankful and relieved that circumstances spurred me into leaving when I did. It wouldn't have been an easy environment in which to bring up two children.

Looking back, Lily-Anne Stroobach, a friend who was a young reporter in Durban at the time told me, 'I remember Richmond before and after (the unrest) too. From heaven to war zone.' She then went on to say that when she was covering a peace march in Durban, a young black marcher she spoke to said of the conflicts between Inkatha and the ANC: 'When two bull elephants stamp, it is the ground that trembles.' These words struck a chord in her heart and have remained with her to this day. Poor Richmond continued to tremble for many years on.

Of the many people I knew there, I have only recently been in touch with Hugh Rethman, my employer, and

Bev Nicholson, the attorney who rented the house to me. From these renewed contacts, I now know that Mr Rethman remained in practice in Richmond until 2000 but eventually moved to England. He told me that Peggy Bernard lived in the area until the mid-nineties but passed away shortly after moving to the coast and that Eunice Hattingh also died around the same time. They would both have been quite elderly by then. As for Dlamini, he too died after retiring to Ixopo, but I have no idea what happened to Alice or Lindiwe and it would be impossible to find out. Bev Nicholson moved to Pietermaritzburg where he still lives. All of them, as well as thousands of ordinary black, Indian, coloured and white people, endured many years of what must have been severely traumatic stress during the years from 1989 onwards.

For my own part, I am selfishly glad that I can remember the town as it once was; that I haven't had my image of it marred by destruction and violence; that my mind's eye can still see its calm, tree-lined residential streets, the faded gentility of Shepstone Street and the bustling vibrancy of Chilley Street. That is the Richmond my memory recalls. Heaven? Well, maybe not quite, but in the mid 1980s it was a small town with a lively heart and lots of slightly ramshackle charm.

What was it I said in the introduction? 'Sometimes it's hard to see the sunshine through the smog.' I've discovered through writing these recollections of my own life there that sunshine prevails in the end. I am happy I've been able to put the good times back in their rightful place – in the forefront of my memory. As for Kwa-Zulu Natal, I've been back quite recently and it is every bit as beautiful and magical as I remember; the people of the 'rainbow nation' are still warm, vibrant, welcoming and friendly.

Maybe one day I will go back to Richmond again too, but for now I think I'll let my memories suffice. They are good, I am fond of them, and I'd like to keep it that way.

THE END

A brief glossary of typical terms used in South Africa:

Bakkie – pick up truck
Billary – tick bite fever in dogs, lime disease in humans, redwater in cattle
Bundu bashing – Off-road driving
Highveld – the upper escarpment region of South Africa
Howzit – Hello, how are you?
Just now – a little later
Kraal – a small community of thatched huts occupied by Africans.
Lekker – great, tasty, nice, good (whatever you wish that's positive)
Mealies – maize cobs
Mealie meal – maize flour
Now now – in a moment
Pap – porridge made from maize meal
Veld – open fields
Vlees – meat

If you are interested in seeing a few of my very old photos of the farm where we lived in South Africa, you can find them here:
https://vallypee.blogspot.nl/p/african-ways.html

ACKNOWLEGEMENTS

I would like to take this opportunity to thank all those who have read earlier drafts of this book. They are Jude Burt, Rebecca Hislop, Jodie Beckford, Dee Tavener and Paulien Wijnvoord. I valued the feedback they gave me tremendously. In addition, I would like to thank all my readers, especially those who encouraged me to write this sequel to African Ways. Without you, I wouldn't have started it, so in a sense, this is for you. Of special note are Julie Haigh, Margaret Hobbs, Caryl Williams, Patti St Marie Wilson, Sandra McKenna, Colin Pryce and Chris Moore. Lastly, I must mention my wonderful contacts among the Twitter community: Terry Tyler, Peter Davey, Carol Hedges, Lynn M Dixon, Stephanie Parker McKean, Tonia Parronchi and all the lovely authors on the We Love Memoirs Facebook and Twitter pages. Your support and encouragement have inspired me to keep writing.

ABOUT THE AUTHOR

Valerie Poore was born and educated in England, but moved to South Africa in 1981. Following her five years in what is now Kwa-Zulu Natal, she lived in Johannesburg until finally settling back in Europe in 2001. She now lives in the Netherlands and shares her time between her Dutch barge in Rotterdam and a cottage close to the Belgian border.

Val has written several other memoirs. The prequel to this book is African Ways, which was first published over ten years ago. Her other memoirs are as follows:

Watery Ways
Harbour Ways
Walloon Ways
Faring to France on a Shoe

She has e also written two novels:

The Skipper's Child

How to Breed Sheep, Geese and English Eccentrics (although this is part memoir as it is heavily based on her years as a smallholder in England before moving to South Africa, even down to the names of the animals)

All her books are available as both e-books and paperback.

Made in the USA
Coppell, TX
13 June 2021